# THE
# PRACTICAL
# ORNITHOLOGIST

**John Gooders**

THE
# PRACTICAL
# ORNITHOLOGIST

**John Gooders**

All pictures supplied by
Bruce Coleman

Facts
On File

Facts on File, Ltd.
Collins Street
Oxford OX4 1XJ
United Kingdom

British Library Cataloguing in Publication Data
Gooders, John, 1937-
    The practical ornithologist.
    1. Great Britain. Birds. Observation
    1. Title
    598'. 07' 23441

ISBN 0-8160-2363-8

This book was designed and produced by Quarto Publishing plc, The Old Brewery, 6 Blundell Street, London N7 9BH

**Designer** Hazel Edington
**Artists** Peter Bull
David Kemp
Mark Iley
Janos Marffy
Maurice Pledger
Paul Richardson
David Thelwell
**Picture Manager** Joanna Weise
**Assistant Art Director** Chloë Alexander
**Editors** Robert MacDonald
Paula Borthwick
**Indexer** Jill Ford
**Art Director** Moira Clinch
**Editorial Director** Jeremy Harwood

Manufactured in Hong Kong by Regent Publishing Services Ltd
Printed by Leefung-Asco Printers Ltd, Hong Kong

# CONTENTS

# FOREWORD

Watching birds comes easily. Primitive man watched birds for his own reasons but, while he sought to understand them to catch them for the pot, he could not have failed to find them fascinating in their own right. He noted their regular appearances and disappearances, their strange antics in spring, their marvellous songs which doubtless he tried to imitate and, above all, he wondered at their powers of flight.

Not surprisingly birds figure largely in primitive art, from the caves at Lascaux and Altamira in Europe, to the rock paintings of Bushmen in the Kalahari and the Aborigines in Australia. And, in the few primitive cultures that survive in our shrinking world, people still refer to birds by their culinary qualities. The people of New Guinea offer a fascinating example of primitive man's relationship with birds. For while birds have been given names such as "Large Eating Bird" and "Small Non-eating Bird", their beautiful feathers are also widely used in symbolic decoration.

### The appeal of birding

Today there is little obvious wildlife around us except birds. That perhaps explains why watching them has become so important to so many people during the 20th century. Certainly, the sport of birding, with its emphasis on the pursuit of birds, can be seen as the sublimation of the hunting instinct. Yet, just like our predecessors, we seek not only to locate and see birds in their natural environment, but also to understand them and their lives.

It is the aim of this book to lead from this fascination to a deeper understanding of the only form of wildlife that has been able to survive in number and variety alongside us. It is a celebration of birds and is written in the hope that the reader will develop his or her own fascination for birds and become a more informed and skilful watcher as a result.

The Crested Tit is one of the least adventurous of British birds. While it is relatively common in Scotland's Spey Valley it has never managed to cross the hills and colonize adjacent Deeside.

# BIRDS AROUND US: INTRODUCTION

Birds vary enormously in size, shape, colour, length of life, habitat, population, food, hunting methods and so on. Since they first appeared about 150 million years ago in the Jurassic period, they have managed to occupy virtually every part of planet Earth. Even in the most hostile of environments, the regions surrounding the two Poles, they manage to utilize some elements of the landscape to their advantage. Indeed some species actually breed within a few hundred kilometres of the South Pole, including the remarkable Emperor Penguin, which incubates its single egg on its feet on the frozen sea during the Antarctic winter.

Birds may range in size from huge Eagles to tiny Wrens yet, I would venture, no one would have any difficulty in identifying any of the world's 8,600 plus species as birds.

One of the most important factors in this apparent uniformity of appearance is the structural requirements of flight. Even the huge

**Left** The Emperor Penguin places its single egg on its feet, where it is incubated by a special fold of skin.

**Above** Ostriches have evolved from flying birds to running birds that avoid danger on foot rather than in the air.

flightless birds that inhabit the southern continents are descended from birds that could fly some time in the distant past. Their loss of flight was a simple adaptation to a particular environment, whether it was to the pampas of South America, like the Rheas, or the forests of Australia, like the Cassowary.

Flight does, of course, make birds the most mobile of all animals and man has always envied them their mastery of the air and the freedom that such mastery bestows. Flight enables birds to take advantage of distant food sources and make lengthy journeys to enjoy seasonal abundance. But all birds, be they migrants or residents, rely on their powers of flight to escape predators and it is

Such different sizes and routines are typical of the variety of ways in which birds live. Yet these are two species that most people know, and which are widely spread through the northern part of our planet. Elsewhere there are birds that live in the most remarkable of ways. There are birds that construct incubators instead of nests; birds that feed on parasites that in turn live on large mammals. There are birds that use echo-location just like bats, and birds that dive 180m (600ft) to the seabed to feed. There are birds that behave like locusts, devouring everything in their path and numbered in their billions, while others are so rare that they may be seen only once in a generation. There are birds that spend their lives at sea circling the globe for years on end and others that fly over the world's highest mountains without the

**Left** Golden Eagles have a home range covering between 2000 and 7000 hectares, which may contain up to 12 different nest sites.

**Below** The tiny Goldcrest builds a nest cup high among the outer branches of a conifer to hold its seven to 10 eggs.

the ability to escape into the air that has enabled them to survive while slower, land-based creatures have succumbed to human predation. Indeed, it was not until the relatively recent invention of the shotgun that man was able to make any serious and deliberate inroads into the populations of most wild birds.

**Bird specializations**
Our fascination with birds is, then, due partly to their ability to live alongside us and partly to their aerial mastery. Along the way they have had to specialize and this, in turn, has led to the development of a huge variety of different shapes and sizes. Golden Eagles soar over remote mountain ranges eyes alert for Ptarmigan or hare. They hold territories that are measured in square kilometres rather than square metres. In a normal season they will lay two eggs, but rear only one youngster, which will take three or four years to reach maturity. The tiny Wren, on the other hand, skulks deep in tangled thickets and lays five to eight, sometimes as many as 16, eggs. Its territory is small, not much larger than a decent-sized back yard, and its young are unlikely to survive more than a few months. It breeds after one year and is lucky to live to be two or three years old.

aid of strap-on oxygen cylinders. There are House Sparrows gradually colonizing the world and Kirtland Warblers restricted to burnt-over Jack Pine stands in a particular area of Michigan.

# GARDEN BIRDS

Though the birds of the world are so variable most of us start our interest in them in our own back yard. We watch them come boldly to the feeders and bird tables in winter. We note the aggressiveness of one, the quiet dominance of another and a general pecking order that ensures that serious fighting is avoided. We see pairs beginning to form as the harsh weather of winter gives way to the lengthening days of spring and we puzzle to tell male from female.

**Distinguishing characteristics**

With some species like the Greenfinch or Cardinal it is easy to tell the sexes apart - males are simply brighter than females - but with others we may have to search for smaller plumage differences. With the Titmice and Chickadees, for example, most species are virtually impossible to sex accurately. The European Great Tit is something of an exception for, while both sexes have a bold black stripe extending down the centre of the breast, that of the male widens out between the legs, whereas that of the female is little wider than on the breast. Thus, with patience, it is possible to tell male from female by this means.

In the case of the American Robin the female has a paler head than the male, but this again needs patience and a little experience to pick out accurately. The European Robin, however, is utterly impossible to sex on plumage characteristics and one must resort to behavioural

features. In late winter and early spring, males and females will often visit feeders together. Sometimes one will adopt a submissive posture that involves lowering the red breast (the female) while the other boldly shows its breast to advantage (the male). As spring develops it is the male that does most of the singing.

Gradually we get used to the birds that visit our gardens. We probably keep a list of birds seen, so that a new garden bird becomes a source of great interest. In the eastern United States the colonizing House Finch frequently visits feeders and may be a new record for the County or even the State. In Britain the Siskin visits feeders only in March and

**Left** Though really birds of heath and hedgerow, Yellowhammers are among the most colourful of the birds that the bird gardener can hope to attract.

**Above** Bird feeders attract a wide variety of different species, especially when there is snow on the ground. Here Great and Blue Tits, Chaffinch, Greenfinch, and the more unusual Brambling and Hawfinch have come to feed.

then only those made of red nylon filled with peanuts. The appeal of listing the birds will quickly lead to extending the garden skywards to include those birds, like the gulls and pigeons, which seldom if ever land, but which use the garden's "air space". At this point one should beware, for it is a short step from noting birds flying over a garden to venturing out to see what birds are present in the local park or surrounding countryside. I say "beware", because becoming a birder can seriously damage other aspects of one's

**Below** Blackbirds, like this female, are regular visitors to suburban bird tables where a wide variety of food will be taken.

**Right** The Siskin is a regular visitor to feeders in March. Usually they prefer pink peanut bags, but this female finds a wire feeder quite acceptable.

life. It can become a passion that is all but impossible to shake off.

### The birder and garden birds

Long before you become a dedicated birder, there is still much, much more to do around the garden or back yard. Already you have noted that different birds feed in different ways. Some come readily to bird tables, others to hanging nut bags. Some can "unwrap" hard-coated seeds, while others can do no more than pick up small morsels. Some will never actually alight on the bird table but will find what they need on the ground, feeding on the fallen crumbs. The secret of good bird feeding is to know what to offer at what times to ensure the greatest range of species. But this

principle applies equally to the whole field of bird gardening, for there is much more than food that can be offered to attract birds.

Water to drink and in which to bathe is almost as important as food and, in drier areas, may prove an even greater attraction. Providing nest sites will ensure that birds will spend the whole summer in the garden. Do not forget nest materials either. Vegetation, that is gardening with birds in mind, can offer food, shelter, roosting sites and, of course, nest sites to birds that will never accept an artificial alternative. Finally, a decent-sized overgrown pond can offer a home to different groups of birds as well as providing nesting materials and an abundant source of insect life to the more regular garden birds.

In today's world the creation of habitats has taken on a new importance. No longer do we need to preserve a particular marsh or meadow when we can recreate another nearby. The bird gardener can do his bit by understanding the needs of birds and by thinking out an active management of what he can, with a little effort, provide.

# FEEDING BIRDS

Warbler

Finch

Wader

Spoonbill

Inevitably the beginner bird gardener will want to feed the birds around the home in winter and it is a simple step to visit the local hardware store and pick up a bag of peanuts. Suspended from a shrub, branch, or washing line these will quickly bring in birds such as the Titmice and Chickadees that habitually cling upside down to feed. Other species may come to feed on the debris dropped from the nut bag, especially if it is made of nylon and eventually bursts.

**Choosing a feeder**

A nut bag seldom lasts as long as its contents and it soon becomes obvious that nylon bags are not the answer. In general they are expensive and short-lived, so that an alternative is required. Fortunately bird feeding has become a minor industry over the past 30 or 40 years and a wider variety of patent feeders is now commercially available. Cheap metal spiral feeders are not advised because it is easy for birds to become trapped by a leg and hang helplessly to die. The best are probably those made of small gauge square galvanized wire. They are sometimes rectangular, sometimes cylindrical, but in each case they have a removable lid that allows topping-up on a daily basis.

There are several advantages in setting up permanent metal feeders rather than convenience net bags. Birds soon get used to a permanent site and a quick check and a regular meal becomes part of their daily routine. A tiny feeder will, of course, need regular refilling to meet the needs of a growing band of clients, so that there is an obvious advantage in a larger feeder that requires filling less often. Sadly no one has yet invented a suspended peanut hopper that replenishes itself, but larger feeders are available, or can easily be made by an amateur handyman. Whatever the size of feeder used you will get more birds if you offer more feeding stations - timid birds cannot afford to waste precious minutes of winter daylight hanging around waiting for the "class bully" to take his fill. So by providing several feeders, even close

**Left** Bills are adapted to different foods or different feeding methods. Warblers snap up insects; Finches crack seeds; Waders probe in mud; Spoonbills sift through ooze.

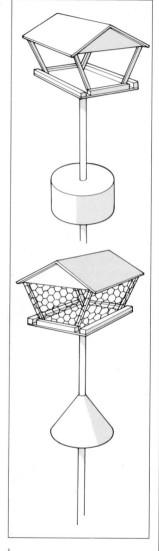

**Above** Bird tables provide feeding opportunities for birds that cannot cope with hanging food dispensers, thus widening the range of birds that will use the garden. The rim prevents food from falling off; a roof protects against rain; a guard deters mice and squirrels; and wire mesh enables small birds to feed while discouraging large ones.

together, you can offer more frequent feeding opportunities both to individual birds and to species. You will, however, need more peanuts and it is surprising just how many your visitors can get through in a winter's day.

Do not offer birds dry-roasted or salted peanuts sold as drink-time nibbles for people - birds do not like them and they are very expensive. Peanuts are not the only food that birds will take, but they are excellent value, high in nutrition and easy to buy, store and serve. The galvanized wire basket will, however, hold all sorts of other bird food from bacon rind and other kitchen scraps to stale cheese and bread.

**Bird tables**
Before long it will become obvious that, while a great many birds are coming to feed, there are still a lot of local species that seldom, if ever, put in an

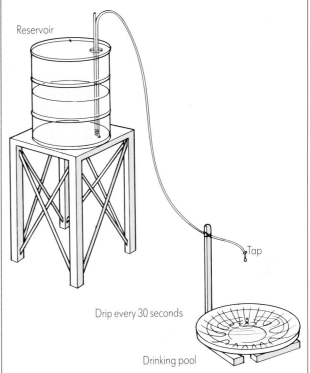

**Above** Water is essential to birds and many different species will come to drink and bathe. Moving water is particularly attractive to warblers and a regular drip system will bring in birds that are otherwise seldom seen in gardens.

appearance. This is the time to diversify into a bird table. Bird tables are neither more nor less than that, but do remember that birds are like young children and are generally messy eaters. Like a high chair, bird tables should have a rim that prevents food from constantly slipping overboard. As rain can turn what looks like a bird feast into a soggy mush, a protective roof is also a good idea. The table should be high enough to deter the local cats and preferably armed with a cone-shaped mammal guard on the supporting post to deter mice. Such a table can be used to offer a wide variety of food, from seeds and bird cakes to pieces of suet and even water.

High concentrations of birds can lead to an outbreak of disease which not only infects the birds but may also be a threat to human health. Tuberculosis commonly infects the more gregarious birds and is not only recorded in many outbreaks each year, but is a regular cause of food

**Above** A seed hopper like this will prove a regular feeding place for species such as these | Red-winged Blackbirds. The large pale-eyed birds are Brewer's Blackbirds.

poisoning in man. Dead and dying birds are not a pleasant sight and, in any case, defeat the whole object of the feeding exercise. Disease is passed on via the birds' droppings and particularly by rodents attracted to food left overnight on the ground. A minimum of hygienic precautions will eliminate the risks of spreading such diseases.

Keep the bird table and the ground below the table and hanging baskets as clean and free from infection as possible. Make a point of moving all feeders, including the bird table, every so often so that the soil beneath does not become contaminated. Above all try to reduce spillage by putting up for offer only what the birds could reasonably be expected to consume in the space of one day.

**Left** A new feeder in a garden quickly attracts birds to feed. Among the first to respond will be the Titmice, like this Great Tit at a terracotta feeder.

**Above** An American Broad-billed Hummingbird feeds on a sugar solution dispensed from a specially designed feeder. Most hummers will take readily to these artificial food supplies.

Though most bird feeding programmes start with a hanging peanut dispenser and a bird table, this is only a beginning. Other forms of hanging feeders can be equally effective. A piece of suet pierced and suspended on a piece of string will bring in most of the birds that regularly feed on peanuts, but at a fraction of the price. Indeed, many butchers are sympathetic to the idea of feeding birds when it is explained to them and will donate the suet free of charge. Suet does, however, quickly become an unsightly and dirty mess when hung in this way, though the birds do not appear to mind. More aesthetically appealing is to select an attractive log and bore holes through it into which suet can be pushed. Suspended from a branch or bird table it makes an appealing feeder that, with care, can be used for "natural" bird

photography. Such disguised feeders will also bring in Nuthatches and Woodpeckers, which do not find hanging baskets totally satisfactory.

**Feeder locations**

The positioning of suspended feeders and bird tables is in itself something with which to experiment. While we do wish to feed the birds and do them good, our aims are not totally altruistic. We provide food to enjoy watching birds and that means placing the feeders where they can easily be seen. For most of us the area outside the kitchen window is as good as any, but at first floor level feeders can actually be attached to the window, or window frame itself. Birds soon get used to feeding within a few centimetres of people and the close-ups provided are a revelation. Some tenants of high-rise apartments have been surprised at just how many birds have been able to find window-box feeders many storeys up over a city centre.

Birds, then, can be attracted to a wide range of different feeders in an equally wide range of different situations. Serious bird gardeners have, over the years, developed an even more impressive range of bird foods, most of which rely on a fat to bind together seeds and bread. Each expert swears by the effectiveness of his or her own cake, but I know of no secret recipe that produces more birds than any other. The important point is to offer as wide a range of foods as possible - particularly of seeds, from sunflower to hemp - so that each species can find what it needs at your banquet.

There are, however, some highly specialized feeders such as those that dispense a sugar solution to Hummingbirds. In some parts of the United States several different species can be seen feeding at the same time from different feeders hung strategically around the house porch. Some come with artificial flowers to draw the birds in, but these are often lost and the birds still come nevertheless.

**Water**

Food apart, water is the next most important substance a bird requires. Most birds drink several times a day and the provision of a drinking place, or bird bath, is a sure way of bringing in extra species. This is particularly true during winter, when natural waters may be frozen solid, but also in arid and drought conditions when the water you provide could make the difference between life and death. Ideally, water should be provided in a shallow bowl with gently sloping edges so that birds can stand in the water to bathe. Most commercially produced fibreglass garden ponds are too steep-sided, though they can be made more acceptable by the provision of a "duck board" sloping into them. However, any depression can be lined with heavy duty polythene to form an adequate bird pool. An inverted lid of a dust bin makes a perfect small pool and all the usual garden birds will be attracted especially if it can be kept filled and ice-free. Some species, such as the Warblers, have no use for feeders but still need to drink and bathe. The water should be kept moving by arranging a very slow, but regular, drip from a height.

**Left** A Song Thrush uses a traditionally designed bird bath to clean its feathers. Though attractive to humans such purpose-built sanitary arrangements are quite unnecessary to birds.

**Below** Bathing is an essential part of feather care for most birds. This Robin is clearly enjoying a thorough soaking.

# BIRD GARDENING

Nest boxes are freely available at most gardening centres, shops and hardware stores. They come in a variety of shapes, sizes and designs and the vast majority are useless. It seems obvious to me that nest boxes should be designed to appeal to birds rather than to people, yet most of those available through retail outlets work on exactly the reverse principle. Birds will occupy boxes that conform to the criteria that they apply to natural holes. They should be out of direct sunlight, that is face northwards in the northern hemisphere and southwards in the southern hemisphere. They should be away from the prevailing winds, that is face eastwards over most of western Europe, though subject to local circumstances. They should be large enough to accommodate a brood of 10 or more virtually adult-sized birds – about 15cm (6in) square in plan. And they should have an entrance appropriate to the size of the bird – that is an entrance hole some 3cm (11/8in) in diameter for most Titmice and Chickadees. Such boxes can be made at home, purchased from national or local bird societies, or via mail order from advertisers in bird magazines. However, there is one other major requirement that applies to all nest boxes: they must be easy to open, for after use at the end of the breeding season boxes should be cleaned out ready for winter roosting and the next breeding season.

**Varieties of nest box**

There are, of course, many other artificial nests than the standard "holed entrance" box. An open fronted box will attract Flycatchers, although some prefer a "holed" entrance with a hole slightly larger than that used by Titmice. A favourite device of my own is to fix an old kettle against a wall for Spotted Flycatcher - it works year after year. Larger boxes can offer a home to Owls, provided they are placed high enough in a tree, or even Kestrels, if they are right at the very top. In

fact any hole-nesting bird is a potential nest box user provided that the right shape and size are offered in the right position. Some bird gardeners have gone to enormous lengths to try to satisfy the needs of particular species. Realizing that the Willow Tit always excavates its own nest hole in a rotten tree stump, one enthusiast filled an ordinary "holed" nest box with expanded

**Left** This Great Tit has adopted a strange, castle-like nest box in which to rear its young, but such elaborate boxes are unnecessary to attract birds.

**Above** Pied Flycatchers take readily to nest boxes and have increased in many areas, where suitable homes have been erected for them.

## Nest box construction

Three easy stages in nest box construction. The use of good quality wood and securely glued joints makes for a weatherproof home for the inhabitants.

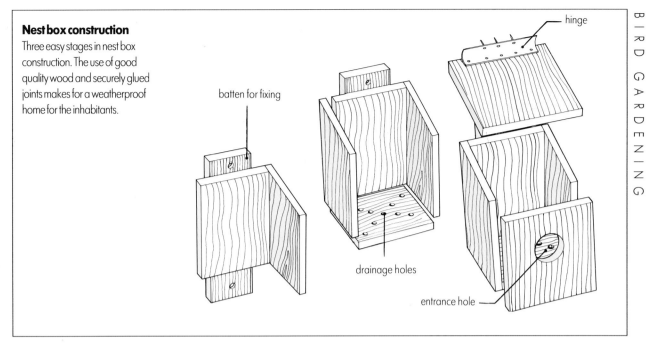

batten for fixing

hinge

drainage holes

entrance hole

polystyrene so that the birds could hack out their ideal home from this soft material. And it worked. Imagination, thought and a good understanding of a particular bird's requirements can bring a great deal of satisfaction if the box offered is a success.

The European House Martin builds a neat gourd-shaped structure of mud beneath the eaves of town and village houses. They can be encouraged by placing a row of specially constructed replicas in similar positions. Barn Swallows nest in barns and outbuildings and the erection of a short, narrow ledge can often encourage them to occupy an otherwise unsuitable site. Even Sand Martins (Bank Swallows) will take to an artificial bank with horizontal oval holes backed by a sand cliff. I have seen one made of concrete against a sandy shingle bank which worked perfectly.

The complete bird gardener will, however, not only be offering food, water and places to nest, but will also attempt to supply everything else a bird needs. Nesting materials may be in short supply and the provision of a dispenser holding soft feathers, sheep's wool and even lichen may attract a good variety of species at the right time of the year. Fallen apples left on the ground during the winter will bring in Thrushes that seldom visit bird tables. Better still, store the apples until winter when little natural food is available.

**Above** Birds, like this Mistle Thrush, often depend on the seasonal abundance provided by fallen apples to help them through the latter part of the year. Each season puts a strain on birds, but none more so than winter, when many die of starvation.

### Alternatives to nest boxes

Actually, there is no limit to what ingenious bird gardeners can do to bring birds into their domains. Planting suitable berry-bearing shrubs such as hawthorn is obvious if the back yard is large enough to accommodate them. Leaving piles of uncleared brushwood offers nest sites to birds such as Wrens. Overgrown tangles in a garden corner may offer a home to Warblers, and so on.

# HOW BIRDS WORK: DESIGNED FOR FLIGHT

One of the most important features of birds is the structural adaptations necessary for flight. The ability to fly makes them not only highly mobile but imposes strict limitations on their diversity, for instance, limiting their size. The heaviest flying birds weigh no more than 18kg (40lb), whereas those that have successfully dispensed with the need to take to the air may weigh several hundred kilograms. There is a complex interrelationship between weight and power that effectively means most birds, along with other flying animals, are small and light in weight.

## Flightless birds

The Ostrich has dispensed with flight by developing long powerful legs and antelope-like feet: It avoids danger not by flying but by running very fast. Other species, notably Rails, have dispensed with flight because of the lack of ground predators on their island homes. Once established on a predator-free island, these already weak fliers quickly adapted to new circumstances in geographical isolation. They have no need of flight. Only during the last century or so have these endemic Rails suffered a decline due to human introductions of alien predators such as rats and cats. The Flightless Cormorant of the Galapagos Islands was able to dispense with flight simply because of the immense richness of the seas around its island home, whereas the world's other Cormorants need to fly long distances to the richest fishing grounds.

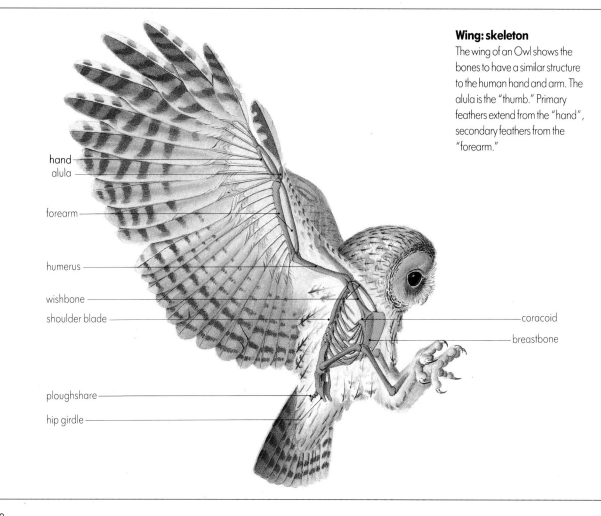

**Wing: skeleton**
The wing of an Owl shows the bones to have a similar structure to the human hand and arm. The alula is the "thumb." Primary feathers extend from the "hand", secondary feathers from the "forearm."

hand
alula
forearm
humerus
wishbone
shoulder blade
ploughshare
hip girdle
coracoid
breastbone

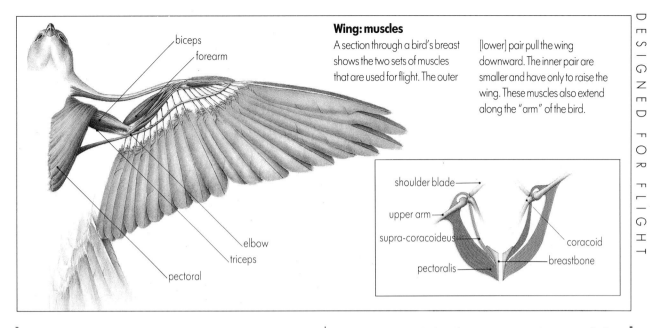

## Wing: muscles

A section through a bird's breast shows the two sets of muscles that are used for flight. The outer [lower] pair pull the wing downward. The inner pair are smaller and have only to raise the wing. These muscles also extend along the "arm" of the bird.

biceps
forearm
elbow
triceps
pectoral

shoulder blade
upper arm
supra-coracoideus
pectoralis
coracoid
breastbone

The Flightless Cormorant propels itself underwater with its huge webbed, paddle-like feet, whereas those other marine fish-eaters, the Penguins and Auks, have developed even further and swim beneath the surface with their wings. In the case of the Penguins this process has been taken to the logical conclusion of flightlessness simply because of the safety of the areas they inhabit around the Antarctic continent and the southern seas. The northern Auks, save for the extinct Great Auk, never developed so far. They are thus not the perfect underwater fishermen that the Penguins have become, nor are they very good fliers. Their wings serve two distinct functions; they are a compromise.

### Why birds fly

Flightlessness has, then, evolved among extra large birds that can outpace or out-fight their enemies; among birds that find their food without travelling huge distances at sea; and among birds that have colonized isolated islands free of predators. It follows that flying birds, that is the vast majority, need flight for just these purposes, that is, to escape enemies, to find food and to travel long distances. Naturally there is a huge variation in the methods by which these needs are met. The average Grouse, for example, uses the power of flight solely for protection and is incapable of sustained long-distance journeys. Gannets on the other hand have few natural predators and rely on their aerial powers to search for and obtain food. The Swifts similarly capture their prey in the air, but also make lengthy migrational journeys to enjoy the long days of summer throughout the year.

Birds are adapted to flight in a number of ways, and their ability to fly has a profound effect on their lives. But flight is, overall, the single most

**Below** The spread wing of a Barn Owl shows the elaborate structure that is required for flight. The small oval feather protruding from the bend of the wing is an anti-stall device called the alula that smooths the passage of air over the wing as the bird comes in to land.

important factor in understanding birds: virtually every aspect of their lives is geared to flight.

**Wing shape**

While all flying birds have a basic wing and feather structure in common, the actual shape of the wing varies enormously. Some birds are highly aerial, fast fliers like the Swifts. Their wings are long and pointed and their streamlined body shape fits their mode of living. Vultures are also highly aerial, but they do not feed in the air and do not require the speed and agility of the Swifts. Their long, broad wings enable them to circle slowly overhead, watchful for signs of carrion, and their stalling speed is extremely low.

Hummingbirds have extremely long and attenuated wings that beat so fast they produce the audible hum which gives them their name. They are the complete aerial masters, capable of hovering before a flower to feed and even of flying backwards. Their remarkable abilities stem, in part at least, from their unique ability to use both the

**Above** Most of the world's birds can fly, but none fly as far as the Arctic Tern, which covers 22,000 miles a year on migration alone. Just how far these birds fly in a year is a mystery, but it is certainly several times the mileage of the average car.

downsweep and the upsweep of the wings to generate power.

**Feather functions**

This contrast in wing shapes is best exhibited by birds that live totally different types of life. Grouse, for example, are ground-dwelling land birds and escape predation by concealment rather than flight. When forced into the air, their rounded wings produce a sudden burst of acceleration and they then glide low over the ground before alighting. In sharp contrast the wings of the Albatross are long, narrow, gliding wings which support the bird with barely a flap. In this case propulsion is provided by the force of the wind and the upcurrents in the oceanic wastes that it inhabits.

While the feathers of the wings and tail provide lift and propulsion in flight, these are not their only functions. In some groups, such as Waders, they are boldly marked with bars that serve as identification and contact marks in fast-flying flocks. Some species, notably the Pennant-winged Nightjar, even have specially extended feathers that protrude from the wing and are part of territorial and nuptial displays. While such appendages are unusual and would clearly seem to impede a bird in flight, tail streamers are comparatively commonplace. The tail of the resplendent Quetzal of South America is three times as long as the body; and nearer home the Skuas have all evolved streamers in breeding plumage.

Body plumage does not act only as an insulator. Most birds are coloured, and for a variety of reasons. Many are camouflaged so as to avoid predators. Others are boldly coloured to attract mates or defend territories. Others have patches

**Below** The long, narrow wings of the Laysan Albatross are ideally suited to using the air currents generated by ocean waves to create lift. The similarity to a glider is not accidental.

**Right** The Peregrine Falcon is the epitome of power and grace. It is the equivalent of the fighter plane and, from its prey's viewpoint, just as menacing.

of bright colours that enable individuals of the same species to recognize one another. The family of bee-eaters all look remarkably similar and are best identified by the areas of bright colour about the head. We find such colour patches useful to name the various species, and there is no reason to suppose that the birds themselves do not utilize them for similar purposes.

## Power-to-weight ratio

Though feathers may be the most obvious adaptation to flight, in fact the whole structure of birds is geared to providing the best power-to-weight ratio. Their bones are thin-walled and hollow and, wherever extreme strength is required, they are honeycombed. Muscle is reduced to a minimum. In fact the only really substantial areas of muscle on a bird are the flight muscles located on either side of the sternum or breast-bone. These muscles, the breast of a chicken, are divided into two sets, the upper and larger which pulls the wing downwards on the propulsion stroke, and the lower which raises the

wing ready for the next beat. This is the bird's "engine-room", the necessary muscle to maintain powered flight, which may account for half its total weight. In birds that glide, rather than beat their way through the air, these muscles may be reduced, while in some flightless birds they are virtually absent altogether.

All of a bird's other internal organs are reduced in size according to this weight reduction axiom. The digestive system, for example, is remarkably speedy and can deal with food, extracting the useful and discarding the waste, in a matter of minutes rather than hours. The female's ovaries form eggs extraordinarily quickly. A bird simply cannot afford the luxury of carrying around its young within its body for any length of time. The weight of a clutch of eggs would prove too much of a hindrance, impede its feeding ability and make it more likely to fall prey to predators. The system of laying eggs in a nest is ideal for flying animals that need to rear large numbers of young each year to maintain their numbers.

# FEATHERS

Birds are covered with feathers that evolved from the scales of their reptilian ancestors. Feathers vary according to their function. The Penguins, for example, have a waterproof covering of seal-like hairs that form a "fur" to insulate them in the cold waters they inhabit. Their plumage is a marked contrast to that of the Ostrich, whose elaborate plumes serve a different function.

**Types of feather**

The feather is an acknowledged measure of lightness: "light as a feather" we say. Yet it is also the finest of insulators. The feathers of the wings that propel them through the air are both extremely light and extremely strong. The shaft of a primary feather is hollow, flexible, but very difficult to snap. It is bordered by an interlocking series of barbs that forms an effective vane. When a bird's wing is pulled downwards, the individual flight feathers overlap to form a continuous area. On the up-beat the feathers twist and open to allow air to pass freely between them.

The primary feathers (the long feathers on the outer joint of the wing) vary in number between nine and 12: they are the major propellers, the means of movement. The flight feathers on the

**Below** A hovering European Kestrel uses its long, angular wings to maintain its stationary position relative to the ground. In fact it is moving through the air by facing into the wind. Kestrels find it virtually impossible to hover in a dead calm.

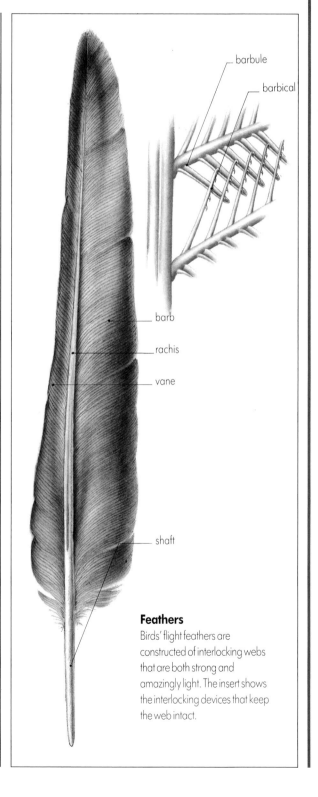

barbule

barbical

barb

rachis

vane

shaft

**Feathers**

Birds' flight feathers are constructed of interlocking webs that are both strong and amazingly light. The insert shows the interlocking devices that keep the web intact.

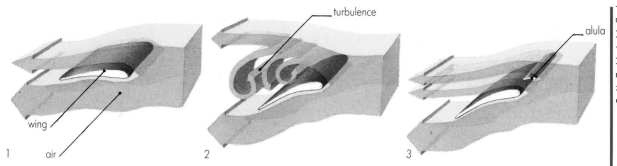

turbulence

alula

wing

1  air

2

3

## Mechanics of flight

In normal flight (1) the air passes smoothly over the wing. When angled to slow down (2) the air creates turbulence over the upper wing and leads to stalling. This problem is overcome by raising the alula (3) to ensure that even at slow speeds air continues to pass smoothly.

**Above** Feather care is an essential part of a bird's existence. Migrants, like this Whimbrel, must ensure that their flight equipment is in perfect working order before setting out on lengthy journeys.

example, may have up to 32 secondary feathers.

Modern aircraft fly at extraordinary speeds, but they still have to slow down to land. The trouble is that these two requirements conflict to a considerable degree: the result has been the system of flaps that alter the geometry of the wing on a modern airliner. While fast flight requires narrow wings, slow flight requires a larger surface area. Without larger wings the plane would either have to land unacceptably fast or it would stall. Birds have their own built-in anti-stall device in the form of a bastard wing. These stiff feathers grow from the bird's vestigial thumb and have the effect of smoothing out the flow of air over the wing and reducing stalling speed.

### Why birds moult

But, just as airliners have to be taken out of operation for regular servicing, so do birds have to take time off to replace worn and damaged feathers. This process is called moulting. Some birds, such as the Ducks and Geese, actually dispense with all their flight feathers at once and may be quite flightless for days or even weeks while new ones are grown. Some of the highly colourful male Ducks even change into a special camouflaged plumage, similar to that of their mates, during this highly dangerous period. This is called their eclipse plumage. Ducks and Geese can get away with this strategy by obtaining their food while swimming safely on water out of reach of most predators. But most birds moult their flight feathers gradually over a period of several weeks, discarding the primaries sequentially from each wing starting with the innermost.

inner joint, the secondaries, provide lift, to keep the bird airborne. The feathers of the tail help to provide lift, but also act as a rudder and airbrake. The structure of both secondaries and tail feathers is similar to that of the primaries, though they are generally less stiff and more pliable, to suit their function. Both groups are also more variable in number, between different species, than the primaries. The long-winged Albatrosses, for

# ANATOMY

**Above** The huge tearing bill of the White-tailed Eagle is capable of dealing with much larger prey than it could catch for itself.

**Right** The narrow, serrated bill of the Red-breasted Merganser is perfectly adapted to gripping slippery prey under water.

Birds can be divided into a large number of categories on the basis of their food. Indeed they are adapted to take a wide variety of foods. Some are remarkably conservative in their feeding habits, like the Crossbill, which has a bill specially adapted to opening tough pine cones and extracting the seeds. Presented with a bird, an ornithologist can tell a lot about its life simply by studying its bill and its feet. It may, for instance, have a thin insect-eating bill, or a wide gape indicating that it catches its insect food in the air. It may have the long probing bill of a wader such as a Godwit or Curlew, or the thick chunky bill of a Grosbeak suited to cracking hard nuts. Eagles have sharply hooked bills suitable for tearing flesh, though prey is invariably taken with the sharp clasping talons. Ospreys have specially serrated talons suitable for grasping slippery fish, which they hunt by swooping down to the surface of the water from the air. Another fish-eater, the Red-breasted Merganser, has a serrated bill for similar reasons. Woodpeckers have chisel-like bills, Spoonbills along with many Duck have sifting bills, Herons' bills are dagger-like and Hummingbirds' fine pipe-like tubes. Each is adapted to a particular food source. But other birds are all-rounders, capable of taking any opportunity that presents itself. Starlings are particularly good examples of all-rounders, a fact which helps to explain their extraordinary world-wide success.

### Feet and legs

Just as their bills vary according to food, so do birds' feet vary according to their habitats. Ducks have webbed feet and Grebes semi-palmated (partly webbed) ones. Jacanas, often called lilytrotters, have long toes to spread their weight over floating aquatic vegetation, while the foot of the Ostrich has been reduced to two toes suitable for running. Woodpeckers have an unusual arrangement of two toes pointing forward and two back. Such an arrangement makes a set of climbing-irons, ideally suited to clambering over

walking and grasping a simple perch, though keen bird gardeners will know that Titmice sometimes grasp food in their feet like a bird of prey. Yet even among this group of "normal" footed birds there are enormous variations of structure. Pipits and Wagtails have the claw of the hind toe enormously extended as an aid to balance while walking on flat ground, which they do a lot. Ptarmigan, which live at high altitudes and low temperatures, not only have a solid walking foot, but one that is completely feathered to provide insulation against the cold.

### Bill-feet combinations

It is, however, when we consider combinations of bills and feet that we can find out most about

**Below** The powerful, heavy bill of the Blue Grosbeak is perfectly suited to cracking the hard shells of large seeds. In autumn large flocks often gather in sorghum fields.

the rough bark of trees and, with the specially stiff tail, creating a tripod from which to hack forcefully in its wood-pecking activities.

Many shorebirds have long legs, enabling them to wade into deep water in search of food. Few are as long as the Stilt's, which trail out behind in flight and seem remarkably inconvenient when they have to be folded up while the bird incubates its eggs. Swallows and Martins have tiny legs and feet suited to grasping a thin perch, but no more. Swifts have even smaller feet, with all three toes pointing forward, but armed with sharp claws for clinging to rough surfaces.

The "normal" foot of the average perching bird consists of three toes pointing forward and one backwards. It is an "all-round" foot suited to

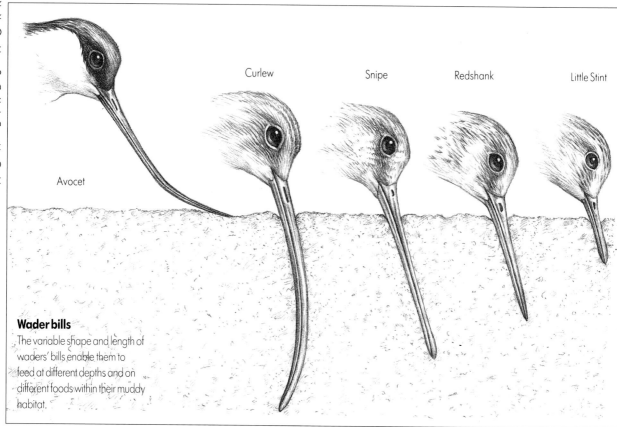

Curlew    Snipe    Redshank    Little Stint

Avocet

**Wader bills**
The variable shape and length of waders' bills enable them to feed at different depths and on different foods within their muddy habitat.

particular birds. As we have seen, birds of prey catch their food in their feet, but use their bills to dismember it into edible-sized pieces. There is thus an enormous difference between the bill-feet of, say, a Golden Eagle and one of the smaller insectivorous falcons. Similarly, although both Osprey and Bald Eagle hunt for fish, their techniques and size of prey vary enormously. The Osprey dives for fish from a height and must be able to rise from the water carrying its prey. Such fish are thus proportionately small and the Osprey needs only a small sharp bill to tear off pieces to eat. Bald Eagles are largely carrion eaters and, when they go fishing for themselves, they simply stand watch over a salmon-rich shallow and do little more than pounce on a fish that lands awkwardly. Such fish are often huge and it takes all the bird's strength to wrestle it from the river. A tough and powerful tearing bill is required to deal with the double problem of large prey and tough-skinned carrion.

One of the most difficult bill-feet combinations to understand and interpret is that of the Flamingo. This strange bird actually feeds on algae that it sieves from the shallows by pumping water through a well developed set of filters that line its bill. It also feeds with its bill held upside down, literally on its head. A Flamingo's legs are extremely long, indicating that it feeds by wading in deep water. Yet because it has such long legs, it also has an extremely long neck so that it can reach the shallow mud among which it spends most of its time. Of course, Flamingos do feed in deep water, but they are quite capable of swimming and even regularly up-end, in a duck-like manner, to reach the bottom to feed. It is all very peculiar, but then Flamingos are rather peculiar birds in other ways too.

Many other birds, that have highly specialized foods or feeding techniques, are also peculiarly adapted. In fact, the more specialized a bird becomes, the more unusual its anatomy. While most North American Hummingbirds have long, tube-like bills to suck nectar from living flowers, none can compare with the endowment of the Sword-billed Hummingbird. This bird inhabits the

South American Andes and has a bill almost as long as its body. In fact, a botanist, working on the flowers of the Datura with their extremely long corollas, predicted the existence of such a Hummingbird before it was actually discovered.

While many of the strangest birds tend to inhabit tropical climes, a few do venture into temperate latitudes. The Snail Kite of Florida, for

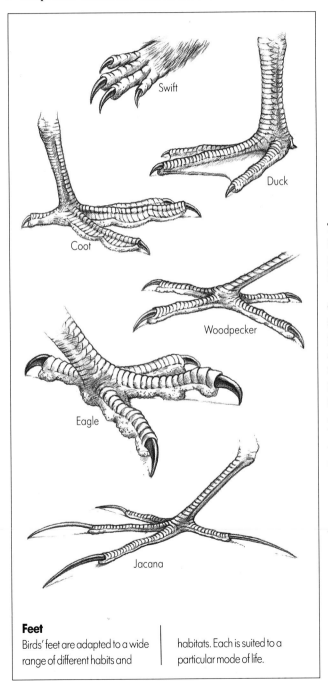

**Feet**
Birds' feet are adapted to a wide range of different habits and habitats. Each is suited to a particular mode of life.

**The Flamingo**
Flamingoes feed with their head upside down and bill pointing backward. Rows of lamellae along the edge of the bill sift algae from salty water.

example, has a tiny winkle-picker of a bill even smaller than that of the Osprey. It is used solely for prying giant Pomacea snails from their shells. Anyone who has seen one of these snails will realize that each individual is a really substantial meal. Also confined to the south-eastern United States, though found in many parts of the tropics as well, is the curiously "deformed" Skimmer. This black and white, Tern-like bird is unusual in having the lower mandible considerably longer than the upper. It feeds in a quite unique way by flying low over water skimming the surface with its extended mandible and grabbing small fish attracted to its "wake". In fact it often flies back along the same line to collect fish that have gathered during its first passage.

The bird's anatomy may be geared to flight and most are thus relatively small and light in weight, but the variety of shapes, forms, colours and behaviour patterns is more than sufficient for a lifetime of dedicated watching and study.

# THE BIRD'S YEAR

The vast majority of birds work, like ourselves, on a regular, repeated annual cycle that is considerably more complex than the "birth, copulation and death", described by T.S. Eliot as the facts of life. Some species, such as those that breed on or near the Equator, may breed all year round simply because the plants on which they feed bloom and fruit randomly through the year. Similarly some tropical seabirds breed at 10 month intervals, so that the actual timing of breeding changes from year to year. But for most birds, certainly in temperate climes, life is geared to the changing seasons.

Bird-watchers talk of spring and autumn migration, of the breeding season and of winter visitors, but such seasonality does not necessarily correspond with our own sense of season. Spring migrants usually do arrive in spring, but for birds in temperate North America and Europe spring can mean anything from late March till the end of May. Even so, the spring migration of European White Storks takes place in January. Similarly, autumn migration can begin as early as mid-July and last through to early November. The peak period for departing Warblers is August - the time that most of us think of as the height of summer

**Above** Yellow Wagtails are summer visitors to Britain and Europe that make huge | trans-Saharan migrations to winter among the marshes of the Sahel.

and the peak holiday season. If the breeding season is summer then what of the Crossbills that breed in January and February? Nevertheless, there is a definite structure to the life of the average temperate-dwelling bird.

### The seasonal routine

Taking the average summer visitor to our northern lands we find that it will spend winter around the Equator and move northwards in the latter part of our winter to arrive at its breeding site, say in our garden, from mid-April onwards. The male will arrive first and quickly establish a territory, which it will defend by displaying to its neighbours and by singing. The female will arrive a week to two weeks later and will seek out a territory-holding male. Display will lead to mating and nest-building.

**Below** Female Crossbills often breed long before the snow has melted. For this bird summer | may well begin as early as February – a seasonal adaptation to its food supply.

Eggs will be laid, usually early in the morning, until the clutch is complete. They will then be incubated - for some two weeks in the case of a Warbler - and the chicks will hatch naked and helpless. The youngsters will be fed and brooded for a further two or three weeks until they are able to fly and will remain "in care" for a further few days before drifting away. Some species will then go through the whole performance again to rear a second brood.

This comparatively straightforward process takes some 40 days. That is, say seven days to establish the pair, mate and form the eggs inside the female; a day or so to build the nest; 14 days incubation; 16 days for the young to fledge; and three days of post-fledging care. So, for a pair of birds that have found each other by 1 May, breeding could be over by the second week of June. Of course, many things could happen to upset this schedule. The nest could be destroyed, one of the pair could die, the chicks could fall victim to a predator or the weather; but certainly by the second week of July there is a flush of young Warblers appearing in areas where they do not breed. Such movements could be regarded as the start of autumn migration.

### Feeding for survival

One of the essentials for migration is fuel for the long journey to come. So the bird feeds voraciously on the plentiful supply of insects and fruit available at this time. Many small birds actually double their weight before setting off on a flight that may last 40 hours of non-stop flying over the sea, desert or both.

Imagine a small bird weighing less than 15g (1/2oz) flying northward on a journey of some 5,000km (3,000 miles) in spring; building a nest and laying its own weight in eggs; incubating these for two weeks, but still finding enough time to feed itself; then feeding a voracious brood of youngsters who, by the time they are ready to fly, are eating more than the adult itself; then feeding up to double its weight; and finally setting off to fly a return journey of the same distance again; all within a period of 12 weeks. Such a schedule inevitably takes its toll and perhaps fewer than half the birds that set off northwards make the return trip southwards. That some individuals perform this remarkable feat three, four or even five times, hides the fact that only a minority of the young reared in a season live to breed even once.

Understanding the bird's year is essential to all birders simply because, if we hope to see a particular summer visitor, we must see it during a few brief weeks, or wait almost a full year to try again. Similarly, birds that do no more than pass through our area (passage migrants) have to be seen (or missed) during the brief weeks of spring or autumn. Winter visitors from lands further north usually give us a longer period of observation potential, but only the residents are available all the year round. Birds' seasons are a fact of birding life.

# MIGRATION

The ability to fly makes birds the most highly mobile animals in the world. Some species like the Arctic Tern fly from one end of the earth to the other every year; others make more modest journeys, while yet others seldom leave their tiny territories during their entire lives.

It is a fact of geography that large areas of the world are virtually uninhabitable for lengthy periods of the year. The land beyond the Arctic Circle is a hostile place in winter that supports only a few seed-eaters, other vegetarians and the predators that prey on them. In summer, however, everything changes and the tundra becomes full of life while the sun shines 24 hours each day. Many creatures, such as insects, survive in the Arctic to take advantage of this bloom of life by hibernating or spending the winter in a state of suspended development.

Birds, however, with one notable exception (the American Poor-will has been found hibernating in rocky crevices in California) do not hibernate. Instead they migrate from the milder climes to

these rich northern latitudes where they spend the winter. As a result huge numbers of birds - insectivorous passerines and aquatic waders - perform extremely lengthy migrations. The numbers involved are staggering and the losses along the way stunning. But while individuals may die, the species as a whole most certainly benefit. It is axiomatic that if a food source exists some species of bird will have evolved the ability to take advantage of it.

## The mysteries of migration

Migration has always fascinated man, but even as short a time ago as the 18th century the great migration-hibernation debate still raged. That we now know the answer does not mean that we know all about migration - far from it. We know that regular seasonal flights bring birds to our shores. We have a good idea where they winter. We know the routes some of them take and of seasonal variations in such routes. We know that most birds migrate below 1,200m (4,000ft), but that others cross the Himalayas at altitudes where man has seldom been able to penetrate without the aid of bottled oxygen. We know that many migrants are capable of covering long distances non-stop, flying from one day into the next. We know that they take on fuel in the form of fat prior to migrational flights and that some species may even double their normal weight. We know that birds of prey and

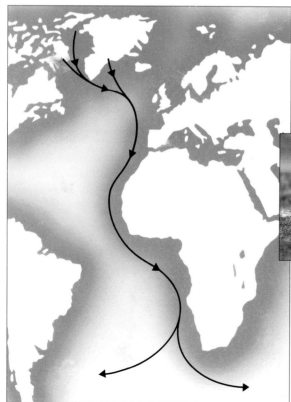

**Left and inset** From their breeding grounds in Greenland and the Canadian archipelago, Arctic Terns make a transatlantic crossing to the coasts of Europe before heading southwards to winter off Antarctica – the longest of any migrational journey.

Storks, because they are dependent on thermals of rising air generated by the heat of the sun on the land, avoid long sea-crossings. And that many other birds migrate on a broad front and are not channelled along particularly favoured routes. These and other aspects of bird migration we know about, but there are many questions that remain unanswered and doubtless many questions

**Left** European White Storks use thermals of rising warm air to aid their soaring migration between Europe and Africa. As thermals are not generated over the sea the birds take the shortest of sea crossings.

**Below** Snow Geese arriving at Klamath Basin National Wildlife Refuge, California. Snow Geese make use of all three major flyways during their migration through North America. In contrast, the diminutive Ross's Goose crosses the Rocky Mountains between its arctic breeding grounds and its winter quarters in California.

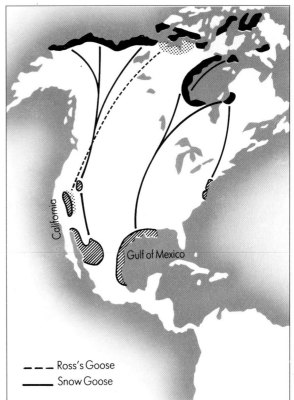

- - - Ross's Goose
—— Snow Goose

that we have not even asked.

Even birds as large and obvious as the Greater Flamingo pose problems. There are, for example, some 10,000 of these birds on the salt lakes of southern Cyprus every winter, but we do not know where they come from. Outside of Europe and North America the problems are immense.

Migration involves untold millions of birds making regular journeys of varying distances throughout the world. Some merely drop down from the mountain tops to the milder climates of the valleys or lower slopes. Such "vertical" migrations may cover only a few kilometres. Others, as we have seen, cover thousands of kilometres every year, much more than the average car, moving from one continent to another.

Inevitably, some birds get lost along the way and turn up in areas where they are completely unknown. In North America the island of Attu in the Bering Straits of Alaska acts as a gathering ground of birders seeking off-course Siberian birds, while in Europe the Isles of Scilly is a similar magnet for birders in search of off-course American birds. These mainly autumn rarities are but the tip of an iceberg of lost migrants. For if an

**Right** Sand Martins and Swallows gather on telegraph wires prior to migration, often in huge numbers.

**Below** Typical of their kind, American Tree Swallows also gather on wires, often in huge numbers.

## Why birds migrate

This destination-based migration, both northwards and southwards, fulfils a remarkably important function. Supposing all the Swallows hatched in North America flew south and then all returned on a random basis to anywhere in the United States. The result could be huge concentrations of Swallows in say the mid-west, and none at all in the east, or west of the Mississippi. Such inefficiency would leave massive unexploited opportunities and staggering scarcity of food and breeding sites in the overcrowded mid-west. By being destination-bound, the Swallow population spreads itself out over the suitable habitat and avoids a natural disaster. In a nutshell, random migration just would not work.

Similar factors decree that individual Swallows winter in the same area, perhaps even the same farmstead, year after year: and that along the way they roost in the same reedbed year after year. This would seem to lead us to the concept of birds having quite definite migration routes and an earlier generation of ornithologists clearly thought that birds were chanelled along mountain ranges and coastlines. It does seem likely that individuals do follow the same route year after year, though maybe a different route in spring to that followed in autumn. Additionally, birds do follow mountain

individual of a species that is unknown can get lost so can individuals of a species that is regular.

Most migrant birds, however, do make their journeys more or less successfully. Leaving the area where they were raised, they fly instinctively to a traditional wintering ground, before returning once more to almost the exact area where they were hatched. Along the way they may stop at places where they have stopped-off before. So the Swallow in the barn may well have hatched there, flown to a farmstead 8,000km (5,000 miles) away and then flown back to the very same barn.

ranges and coastlines, but they also migrate on a broad front and take advantage of such landmarks only when they lead in the right direction.

## Migration and navigation

In the early days of radar development, screens were regularly plagued by "angels", odd echoes that cluttered up the picture and were patently not the enemy aircraft that were being sought. "Angels" turned out to be flocks of migrating birds and it is reassuring to know that modern radar is now "angel-free". However, radar can be adjusted to pick up migrating birds and radar studies have shown just how widespread is bird migration. Coasts may have a funnelling effect, but migration takes place on wide fronts taking no account of narrow sea-crossings or of the world's greatest deserts. Small birds in Europe regularly set off from the coasts of the Mediterranean in autumn to fly non-stop across the sea and then the great Sahara Desert beyond. Such flights must last 40 or more hours and, like a modern aircraft, use up an enormous amount of energy. While aircraft use up aviation fuel, birds use up fat that they have accumulated in a pre-migration feast.

Just how birds find their way is still the subject of hot debate. It is generally agreed that navigation involves the use of the sun during the day and the stars at night, for when it is completely overcast birds become disorientated and get lost. This does, however, mean that birds must have an inbuilt sense of time - an internal clock. There is also evidence that birds respond to the Earth's magnetic field and that the final stage of destination-based migration may be achieved by the sense of smell. Whatever the truth, it is clear that the whole mechanism is, for a majority of bird migrants, completely instinctive rather than learned. For while in species like the Snow Goose, adults lead their young on their first migration, the young of most birds find their own way to a particular spot, in a particular country that is correct for them, but to which they have never been before.

**Left** During their length of the continent migrations, Snow Geese fly in line and V formations, with the leading bird doing most of the work. Most migratory Geese follow a similar routine.

# SONGS AND CALLS

Birds vocalize for a variety of reasons; indeed they are among the most vocal of animals. They sing to proclaim their ownership of a territory, but also utter a whole range of different calls which fulfil a variety of different functions. Alarm calls serve to alert other creatures, as well as their own kind, to the approach of a predator. Outside the breeding season, many species spend much of their time in groups and maintain the composition of the flock with contact calls. Some calls are uttered as threats, aimed specifically at individuals of the same species, or at intruders which may or may not be potential predators. Yet another type of call expresses the bird's excitement. There are calls that are used only during the period of courtship or mating and yet more that are confined to communication between the young and its parents. In a remarkable study, one ornithologist described no less than 57 different calls uttered by the European Great Tit, each presumably with a different meaning. While this should not be regarded as a language, it is a considerably richer repertoire than that of most other animal groups.

## The functions of bird song

Of all of these different forms of vocalization, bird song is both the most obvious and the most pleasing to the human ear. Indeed, it is virtually the only aspect of ornithology that is regularly

**Left** Like most other woodpeckers the North American Hairy Woodpecker uses dead branches to drum its territorial "song." The hollow sound it produces echoes through the woods.

**Above** Ruffed Grouse are unusual instrumentalists that use the sound of their wings beating rapidly – often while perched on a hollow log – rather than their voices to proclaim their place in the sun.

used in literature, showing that even poets are not immune to the charm of birds. Bird song is the means by which males (mainly) proclaim their ownership of a territory and advertise their presence to potential mates. Other animal groups perform the same functions by means of smell or by visual signals. Birds have a comparatively poorly developed sense of smell and only those species that live in open habitats have evolved elaborate visual signals. Cases in point are the Ostrich, which has no song, but exhibits a wonderful semaphore-like wing flapping display that can be seen for long distances across the open African savannahs; the European Great

Bustard which turns itself virtually inside out on the grasslands of Spain and eastern Europe; and the Grouse of the American plains with their elaborate puffed up strutting. But for most birds that live among vegetation, visual signals are pointless and song has immense advantages.

Most bird song is relatively simple and repetitive. There is considerable evidence that many of the standard elements of a bird's song are innate, but that even simple songs may be partially learned. The chipping trill of the Chaffinch, for example, is inherited, save only the final flourish which has to be learned. Songs such as the repetitive chiff-chaff-chiff-chaff and so on of the Chiffchaff are presumably inherited, though there is geographical variation even in so simple a song. However, many birds exhibit a remarkable virtuosity in their songs, with variable phrases and arrangements indicating an apparent choice on the part of the individual. The famed song of the Nightingale is a case in point, though it is perhaps as much the quality of the notes produced by this bird as the actual arrangement of phrases that is responsible for its reputation. Several groups of birds, notably the Nightjars or Nighthawks, produce songs that sound more like machines than birds. They are repetitive, long-lasting and would probably seem quite boring were it not for the secretive and nocturnal habits of these charismatic birds. Similarly many Owls produce a form of hooting that is simple in form, though it is nevertheless a "song". A few birds have even become instrumentalists, using non-vocal sounds to proclaim their ownership of territory. Primary among these are the various species of Woodpecker that drum on dead branches. Individual Woodpeckers have their own dead branches within their territory and, indeed the presence of such "drumming" posts may be an essential ingredient in making an area suitable for breeding. In effect, the dead branch acts as a sounding box, amplifying the rapid beating with the bill into a hollow rattle.

**Top** The Greenfinch's song is a series of chipping notes followed by a harsh rasping. Though far from pleasant it serves the same purpose as the more delightful songs of other birds such as the Nightingale (**middle**).

Curiously, some birds, such as the Starling (**bottom right**), mimic other birds as part of their own song, although it is difficult to see what advantage this serves.

**Above** Ravens have virtually no song, but utter deep, harsh croaks that are both far carrying and distinctive. The calls of all members of the Crow family are very similar and need an experienced ear to separate them.

Other species produce songs by utilizing part of their plumage. Snipe, for example, proclaim their domain by flying in a wide circle overhead and by making a bleating sound produced by vibrating their stiff outer tail feathers through the air in steep dives. Ruffed Grouse in the northern woodlands of North America produce a drumming sound by beating their wings rapidly while standing on a hollow log. These are, however, unusual "songs".

Birds use songs and calls to communicate and, for this reason, they must be clear and readily understood by others of the same species. It is, therefore, difficult to see why some birds mimic others. Many species throughout the world are fine mimics, producing excellent imitations of other birds and a wide variety of sounds. Outstanding is the Australian Lyrebird, which not only produces the songs of other birds that share its range and habitat, but sounds as variable as a tractor, a chain-saw and a falling tree. The European Marsh Warbler is also a noted mimic, though it confines itself to the songs and calls of the birds with which it shares a living space. And even the humble Starling can produce a passable version of other bird songs. It is perhaps not the individual "words", but the "language" itself that matters; in other words it's not the phrases but the accent that picks out one Lyrebird to another Lyrebird. Certainly, when it comes to birds imitating the human voice they do not do it very well, though the wonder is that parrots can say "pieces-of-eight" at all.

## Birders and bird calls

So, just as one bird can recognize another (otherwise the whole business of song would be pointless), so can we, as observers, recognize the songs of birds and identify the species without seeing the individuals responsible. The practical value to the birder of knowing the songs and calls of birds cannot be overstated. A competent birder can walk through a wood full of bird song and identify most of the birds present without seeing a single individual. To the beginner such expertise seems daunting, but by starting with everyday garden birds it is surprising just how quickly one can become familiar with their songs and calls. Even by learning only a handful of the songs of the most common birds one is in a better position to pick out the more interesting species one encounters. If every call or song has to be tracked down to a confirmatory visual contact then a spring walk through a wood becomes more of an ordeal than a pleasure. Gradually, over time, expertise is built up until a wide variety of species can be identified unseen.

Probably the best method of learning bird song is in the company of a knowledgable and understanding friend, actually out and about in the field. Failing this, recordings can be quite useful and listening to them during the long winter evenings is a pleasant and productive way of waiting for spring. Remember, however, to concentrate on the most common species rather than those you particularly want to see. Learn thoroughly, and test yourself by identifying the recordings regularly. Before long you will be moving on from woodland bird song to the calls of contact produced by a variety of species in different habitats.

Shorebirds may seem a difficult group to identify, not because they hide away in dense vegetation, but because they are often seen at considerable distance or in flight and, in any case, they are remarkably similar in structure. A fast-flying group of small waders may produce the rasping "treep" of Dunlin, or the twittering "plick-plick" of Sanderling. In poor light the call may be the only clue to their identity. Most shorebirds have distinctive calls and recognition can alert one to the presence of a species that had not previously been noticed on some overcrowded marsh or estuary.

### Nocturnal calls

With some species, calls are virtually the only contact that one is likely to get without a great deal of stealth, forward planning and local knowledge. Nocturnal species such as the Owls are a case in point. Finding a Long-eared Owl in an extensive conifer forest, for example, is either a matter of luck, or of waiting and listening carefully for the characteristic low, moaning call. Recognizing the calls of the various species of Owl is crucial to locating them, for these birds are never common and actually seeing them is always a time-consuming business. Sadly, many of the Owls call only during the early part of their breeding cycle which is, in any case, usually during the early part of the year. Thus locating, say, a Great Grey Owl involves visiting the northern forests when there is still heavy snow on the ground and transportation is at its worst. Later in the summer these birds are quiet and secretive, making location a matter of sheer good fortune.

Similarly, Nightjars and Nighthawks are birds of the night and location depends on visiting an appropriate habitat at dusk and waiting to hear their characteristic calls. Even then, one is lucky to see the bird, though several species are curious and if one waits in the middle of a suitable hunting area, a bird may well come to inspect. Fortunately, several species regularly come to roads and tracks and may then be caught in a car's headlights. It is, however, essential either to choose a seldom-used road or to try very late at night when traffic is at a minimum.

Songs and calls are, then, an essential method of both identification and location and their recognition is an important ingredient in becoming a birder.

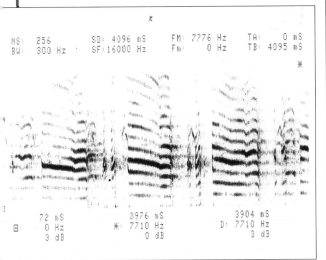

**Above** Sound spectographs are a visual method of recording bird sounds and songs. This is a spectograph of the call of a Kittiwake, which is rendered phonetically as *kitti-wark kitti-wark* and, in words, as Kittywake-Kittywake.

**Below** Most Thrushes produce rather liquid, flute-like songs that are pleasant, but fairly similar. The European Song Thrush has the characteristic habit of repeating each of its highly varied phrases three times. It is not what is said, but how it is said that identifies this bird.

# BIRD NAMES

Identifying, that is putting a name to a bird, is the first essential in learning more about birds. Sadly, it takes only a short interest in birds to find out that different bird books use different names for the same bird. The Tree Creeper in Europe is the Brown Creeper in North America. These variations are frustrating to the beginner and irritating to the experienced.

**Naming systems**

Fortunately there is a more efficient method of identification. Each bird not only has one (or more) English names, but also an accepted scientific name. The Tree Creeper and the Brown Creeper have the scientific name *Certha familiaris*.

The two-part system, or Latin binomial, involves applying a generic name (the first word) and a specific name (the second). Thus the Tree Creeper is a member of the genus *Certhia* and is specifically identified as *familiaris*. There are several other creepers that belong to the genus *Certhia*, but each has a distinctive second, that is

specific, name that identifies it clearly and without confusion. By convention the generic name starts with a capital letter and the specific with a small letter. The names are also printed in italics.

All birds belong to the class Aves. This "class" of living thing is divided into different "orders" which, in turn, are divided into distinct "families". These families consist of different genera which, as we have already seen, consist of different species. Thus, working in the other direction we see that the Tree Creeper is *familiaris* and belongs to the genus *Certhia*. *Certhia* belongs to the family Certhiidae which forms part of the order Passeriformes which is part of the class Aves.

One of the great things about the system of scientific names is that it enables birders from

There are only five species of flamingo in the world, yet they demonstrate just how a group of closely related birds are named in the scientific system.

**Left** Greater Flamingo.

**Above** Chilean Flamingo – both are *Phoenicopterus*.

different countries to converse freely and easily one with another. Latin names overcome the difficulty of paging backwards and forwards through field guides to point at illustrations of birds we wish to discuss with foreigners.

With luck, you have now got the hang of Latin binomials: now comes another minor complexity - Latin trinomials. The basis of our classification system for birds is the species, but there are variations in colour, voice and behaviour that

## Orders and families

The Flamingos of the world may, however, make the business of names a little clearer. Firstly, all Flamingos are placed in the order Phoenicopteriformes. Secondly, they are all members of the family Phoenicopteridae. They are thirdly divided among three distinct genera: *Phoenicopterus*, *Phoeniconaias* and *Phoenicoparrus*. There are, in fact, only five species of Flamingo: Greater Flamingo (*Phoenicopterus ruber*, Chilean Flamingo (*P. chilensis*) (note that

**Far left** Lesser Flamingo at its breeding mound. This bird is placed in a genus by itself – *Phoeniconaias.*

**Left** Andean Flamingo.

**Below** Andean and James's Flamingoes feeding side by side. These two birds are so closely related that they are placed in the same genus *Phoenicoparrus*.

enable us to pick out sub-species. In most cases, this has required detailed comparison of a large range of preserved bird skins in a museum, but some sub-species are sufficiently distinct to be recognizable in the field.

The various populations of the Greater Flamingo are sufficiently different to merit status as sub-species. Indeed, not so long ago, two were regarded as quite distinct species: there was the Greater Flamingo *Phoenicopterus roseus* of the Old World, and the American Flamingo *Phoenicopterus ruber* from the United States, the West Indies and the Galapagos Islands. Today, both populations are regarded as sub-species of a single species, the Greater Flamingo *Phoenicopterus ruber:* the Old World Greater Flamingo being *Phoenicopterus ruber ruber* and the American Flamingo *Phoenicopterus ruber roseus*. If this is all a bit confusing, I make no apologies. Senior ornithologists are continually debating the relationships between different species, sometimes suggesting that they should be placed in one genus, sometimes in another. Like sub-species, it should probably be ignored until the individual finds it interesting.

the generic name can be abbreviated to the initial letter and a full stop on a consecutive mention), Lesser Flamingo (*Phoeniconaias minor*) (note that having only one member, this genus is referred to as being "monotypic", that is a one member genus), Andean Flamingo (*Phoenicoparrus andinus*), James's Flamingo (*P. jamesi*).

# BIRD BEHAVIOUR: TERRITORY

Territory is the mechanism by which birds space themselves out over the available habitat, and the possession, or ownership, of a territory is essential if an individual bird is to breed. In our gardens, parks and countryside, spring sees individual birds, usually males, dividing up the land among themselves. They sing from prominent positions to inform other males of their ownership and display to, or even attack, intruders. Individuals that do not gain a territory are doomed, not only to not breeding, but to a life of continuous harassment, or an existence in marginal habitats not really suited to their needs.

### Territorial essentials

For small birds the essentials of a territory are a choice of nesting sites and a suitable song post or two. Strange as it may seem, relatively few birds actually need a territory large enough to provide all their food. So we can think of the territory as a breeding space, an area where the pair can build their nest, lay their eggs and rear their young in peace. It could be argued that the number of birds is dependent on the number of suitable territories available, though other ornithologists argue that it is the amount of food that determines the population of a particular species. Whatever the answer, it is clear that territory is crucially important to the successful rearing of a new generation.

Territories vary enormously from one species to another. The Golden Eagle needs a range of

**Below** The territories of a Blackbird have been mapped in this suburb. Naturally the birds do not dispute the river, although one lives on an island

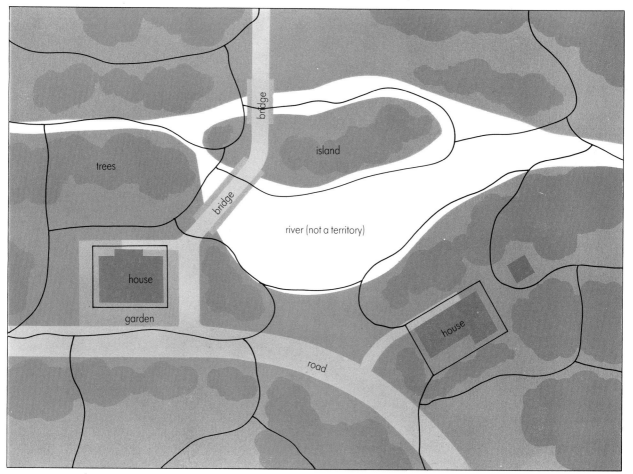

**Left** Male Blackbirds are among the most territorial of birds and will even divide a garden lawn. Just what distinguishes one territory from another in an area so devoid of landmarks requires a glimpse into the Blackbird mind.

**Below** Two Great Crested Grebes come together in a ritualized display that forms an essential part of the breeding routine of these aquatic birds.

**Bottom** Gannets are highly aggressive during the breeding season; an adult attacks a sub-adult.

several square kilometres, with three or four quite separate nest sites, to fulfil its needs. This large and powerful predator defends not only the area around its nest, but also a hunting range that is itself large enough to support a self-sustaining population of grouse, hares and other prey. In contrast, the Gannet defends a territory only as large as it can reach with its bill while sitting on its nest, that is little more than a square metre. These birds too are large and powerful predators, but they find their food away from the nest site at sea.

There are, however, many other examples of territories that fit no pattern at all. Many of the Grouse have communal display grounds, called leks, where males gather, often morning and evening, to attract a mate. Each lek is divided into mini-territories owned and defended by an individual male. The possession of a territory at a lek is essential to any breeding male and the more mature and experienced males will gain the better territories right at the centre of the display ground. At the start of the breeding season there may be much dispute between males as to which holds which territory. Later, when the boundaries are settled, the birds will stand around looking somewhat bored until a female appears on the scene. Her arrival is sufficient to set all the males into a frenzy of display, showing themselves to best advantage in their efforts to obtain her

**Above** Black Grouse live on the edge of conifer forests, but gather to display at special jousting grounds, or leks, in open grassy areas. Each male holds a mini-territory where it raises its tail and puffs itself up to attract a mate.

favours. In this case it is the female that chooses the male and it may happen that the dominant male, at the centre of the lek, is chosen over and over again by different females. In fact, they may even queue for his attentions. Having mated, the females depart to rear the young by themselves. The advantage of the system is that, within his tiny territory, each male is a king and his love-making will not be disturbed.

**Competing for territory**

Outside the breeding season many birds join in flocks and co-exist quite happily, but some maintain a territory throughout the year. The European Blackbird is a good example, for while many northern populations migrate and roam their winter quarters together, those that are resident in milder climes are aggressive throughout the year. Competition among these

Blackbirds is fierce and boundary disputes occur all year round. If one individual dies, its place is quickly taken by another, which has to learn exactly where the boundaries have been drawn. The only way to do this is by trial and error; so the newcomer pushes outwards from the centre of its newly found territory until its neighbours weigh in with vigorous bouts of song and display. It is quite normal to see two male Blackbirds walking side by side across the garden lawn, their progress broken from time to time by towering flights and disputes. The line along which they parade is the boundary between the two territories and even a marginal trespassing will elicit a response from the rightful owner.

The value of such traditional territorial boundaries may be important, not only to the individual, but also to whole populations of birds. In 1962-3 the British Isles experienced one of its coldest winters in recorded history. The countryside was covered with snow, ponds were frozen solid and millions of birds died. Such disasters are, however, not unknown and birds have shown that they are quite capable of recovering from major population crashes. With the coming of spring everyone expected that the survivors would enjoy a bumper breeding season by having the usual amount of food to share between fewer individuals. Yet, strangely, the smaller population actually had a worse than normal breeding season. Instead of mating, nest-building and getting on with rearing young,

Blackbirds spent almost the whole of the summer fighting and displaying. What had happened is that so many individuals had perished that the communal memory of traditional territory boundaries had been lost. The birds simply did not know where one territory ended and the next one began; so they fought. Instead of a recovery, the Blackbird population barely managed to sustain itself until the next year.

**Left** The European Robin is among the most aggressive of all birds in defence of its territory. This bird is attacking a stuffed Robin that has been set up to provoke displays that make much of the red breast.

**Below** The Capercaillie is a huge turkey-like grouse of the dense conifer forests of Europe. Males have elaborate displays, but are also highly vocal in their efforts to attract a mate.

# NESTS

It is easy to think of a bird's nest as a simple, neat, cup-shaped structure made of grasses, lined with a little wool or a few feathers and placed among the twigs of a tree or shrub. In fact, many birds do construct such a nest in which to lay their eggs and rear their young. But just as birds vary in size, colouration, food and habitat, so do their nests vary enormously. Some are intricately woven, miniature masterpieces of construction, with secret entrances and the capacity literally to expand to accommodate a growing family. Others are mere depressions in the ground, totally devoid of lining or decoration. The basic requirement of any nest, be it complex or simple, is that it holds the eggs and young safely.

## Nesting tactics

With safety as the key, we can more readily understand the various tactics that individual species of birds have evolved in the construction of their nests. The nest is only one factor in the breeding equation. Others are the colour of the adult, particularly the adult that performs the incubation; the colour of the eggs; and the colour of the young. If we take a bird that lays white or lightly coloured eggs, then the other variables must, in some way, compensate for their conspicuousness. Though this ignores the implications of the old conundrum, "which came first, the chicken or the egg?" - that is, which of our variables is the dominant? - it does help us to understand how birds' nests work.

The bird that lays white eggs has various options open to it to protect its embryonic young. It could lay them out of sight in a hole, it could construct a domed nest, or it could lay them quite openly and cover them with its own highly camouflaged plumage. In fact, various birds have taken up all three options. Woodpeckers excavate holes in trees, Kingfishers holes in banks, and Storm-petrels holes in the ground or rock crevices. The Wren has adopted the second tactic by constructing a domed nest, while Nightjars and Nighthawks rely on their own amazing camouflage to cover their white eggs laid on the ground.

Taking the other extreme, of birds that lay highly camouflaged eggs, there is hardly any type of nest construction that is unsuitable though laying camouflaged eggs in a dark hole not only has no advantage but, because they are difficult to see, may actually be a disadvantage. Clearly, camouflaged eggs are best suited to birds that nest

**Above** A pair of Song Thrushes at their sturdily built nest constructed of grass stems reinforced and lined with mud. These birds will frequently build one nest on top of another, but never reuse an old nest.

**Right** A Robin feeds its six-day-old youngsters in a similar nest, but one which is lined with grass stems.

The camouflage of the small Plovers is highly disruptive and effective, yet the nest and eggs bear a marked similarity to those of the boldly white Little or Least Tern. In fact, while Terns lay camouflaged eggs mainly on the bare ground, they are very gregarious and for the safety of their nests rely on aggressive communal displays to drive away predators.

With cup- or platform-nesters the first ingredient is to ensure that the nest itself is well hidden and camouflaged. The delicate, lichen-covered nests of some of the Finches are not only delightful, but highly effective in avoiding the eye of predators. Birds such as these are often quite boldly coloured, but the female can be dull in comparison with her mate and, therefore, a more effective nest cover. It is not surprising that where one member of a pair is more dully coloured, it is

**Above** The European Golden Oriole builds its nest suspended between the arms of a horizontal fork, high in a large tree. The colourful male, illustrated here, is surprisingly difficult to see when perched.

**Right** The Ringed Plover lays its eggs on bare ground where they are protected by their highly cryptic coloration.

openly on the ground or to birds that build open nests in vegetation and which, being brightly-coloured themselves, must abandon their eggs to protect themselves from danger.

The eggs of ground-nesters are often so well camouflaged that the addition of nesting material would actually reduce their effectiveness. It is quite dangerous to search for such nests because of the danger of stepping accidentally on the eggs and many nests are destroyed in this way every year. Yet even with such an effective form of concealment there are minor tactical variations.

that bird that performs, if not all then at least most of, the incubation duty.

### Non-nest builders

Ground-nesters apart, there is one other group that constructs no nest at all. These birds simply take over the disused nests of other species and, with little or no repair work, lay their eggs in another's home. Several birds of prey fall into this category, but one species is quite remarkable. The Red-footed Falcon is a gregarious summer visitor to eastern Europe that utilizes nests vacated by

Rooks. In general Rooks breed early and the Falcons arrive late. Sometimes, however, perhaps because of a particularly hard winter, the Rooks postpone breeding for a week or two and the Falcons arrive to find young Rooks still present in the nests. Inevitably battles ensue, for the Rooks are reluctant to leave and the Falcons are aggressive in their attempts to persuade them.

### Nest construction

Just as the tactics of nest site selection and nest placement vary widely, so too do the methods of construction. Some birds nest on the ground in splendid isolation, while others do so gregariously, with nests packed tightly together. Some excavate a hole away from it all, while others prefer to honeycomb a bank with nest holes cheek by jowl. Some hide their dainty little nesting cups in the base of a bush or beneath a clump of grass, while others build packed together for all to see among the highest branches of the tallest trees. Some

birds weave their nests from fine grasses and mosses held together by spiders' webs. Others plaster the structure together, grasses and mud forming a primitive reinforced "concrete". Some use the same nest site year after year, gradually adding to the original to form a veritable mountain of vegetation, while others seem to be content with a handful of sticks almost thrown together.

Frankly, I've always found the nesting habits of birds that make do with the skimpiest of nests something of an enigma. The Pigeons and Doves are prime examples, for they seem almost unconcerned for the safety of their eggs. A few twigs wedged together to form a platform and bingo, they lay their eggs. Breaking all the rules these are boldly white and obvious to any predator. While the birds themselves are not boldly coloured, neither are they camouflaged.

Another strange, though more easily explained, nesting tactic is that adopted by many of the Grebes. These are among the most aquatic of all

**Right** Wrens often choose bizarre nesting sites, like this one inside a barn, tucked behind a woolly hat. The yellow gapes of the young act as signals that trigger the adults to provide food.

are white with, in most species, some sparse speckling. While the Barn Swallow constructs a neat cup against the wall of a barn or outbuilding, bringing individual pellets of mud to be reinforced with grasses, several other species build either complete globes or flask-shaped constructions beneath horizontal surfaces. In all cases the art of construction involves waiting for one course of mud "bricks" to dry before adding the next. This, in turn, means that the birds must have a reliable source of mud fairly close to hand. In areas with summer rain, the birds may rely on mud formed by puddles, but in dry areas a pond, stream or river nearby is essential.

Finding out about the nests birds construct can be both time-consuming and fascinating, but it can also be dangerous. When inspecting a nest, obey the law and ensure that your enjoyment has not left tell-tale signs that would draw the attention of predators to what is intended as a safe hideaway for the most important part of a bird's life.

**Above** The nest of the Long-tailed Tit is a masterpiece of grasses and lichens bound together with spiders' webs, which expands as the large brood of chicks grows in size.

**Right** The Common Buzzard, like so many birds of prey, uses the same nest over and over again, decorating it each time with sprigs of fresh green vegetation.

birds, finding everything they need in the waters on which they live. The nest consists of a floating pile of vegetation anchored to some emergent vegetation or overhanging shrub. Like an iceberg, the structure is considerably larger below the water than shows above and is essentially a floating compost heap. As the water level varies, so the nest rises and falls with the flood, an important safety feature when the fragile eggs are no more than an inch or two above the water line. But, being composed of vegetation, the pile quickly starts to decay and generate heat just like a garden compost, so the eggs are warmed in a natural incubator. Like other birds, Grebes incubate their eggs, but when they leave the nest, the eggs are covered with vegetation from the rim of the nests. This hides the eggs from predators and, incidentally, stains them a mottled camouflage brown.

The Swallows and Martins are divided between hole-nesters like the Sand Martin or Bank Swallow, and mud-builders like the Barn Swallow. Their eggs

# EGGS

The egg is the means by which birds produce embryonic young without being so weighed down that they are unable to fly efficiently. Many small birds lay their own weight in eggs to produce a full clutch. Were females to carry around such a load prior to giving birth to living young, their powers of flight and feeding ability would be seriously impaired. So the egg is another adaptation to flight.

**Left** During the pesticide fiasco of the 1960s, Peregrines were seen to eat their own eggs – shells were so thin that the birds were feeding on the contents of broken shells.

**Above** Like all other Plovers, Killdeer lay well camouflaged eggs that are well suited to the dry grassy plains these birds prefer.

### Smallest and largest

Eggs vary enormously in size, number and colouration. The largest egg in the world is produced by the Ostrich and weighs in at about 1.4kg (3lb). It is the world's largest single cell, yet it is dwarfed by the egg of the now extinct Elephantbird of Madagascar, which produced an egg of some 11kg (25lb) - about the same as 200 chicken eggs. Yet this massive egg weighed only two to three percent of the weight of the bird that produced it. In contrast the New Zealand Kiwi lays a single egg that is almost a third of its own weight. Hummingbirds lay the world's smallest eggs, with the Cuban Bee Hummer producing an egg of only a few hundredths of a gram.

Many birds lay one egg each day until their clutch is complete, but most birds cannot count. Thus if eggs are regularly removed from the nest the female will be induced to lay more than normal in her efforts to make up a full clutch. As a result, gamebirds such as the Pheasant can be robbed by gamekeepers and the eggs placed under a broody hen or in an artificial incubator, so increasing the number of young that can be reared for sport. A single hen Pheasant may, by this method, be persuaded to produce up to 30 eggs in a season. Yet the tiny Goldcrest produces a clutch of 10 eggs, weighing one-and-half times its own body weight, without any artificial encouragement at all.

While some birds such as the Pheasant and Goldcrest produce large clutches of eggs, others produce much smaller clutches but are capable of rearing more than one brood in a season. Residents generally start breeding earlier and finish rearing later than summer visitors. Some of the more common Thrushes, for example, produce three, four or even five clutches of eggs each year. At four or five eggs per clutch, a total of 20 or more eggs may be laid in a single season. Other species, such as the Fulmar, produce only one egg each year, yet they still manage not only to maintain their numbers but enjoy a boom population

Just as birds' eggs vary in size and number, so too do they vary in colour and shape. In some cases it is easy to see why the eggs of a particular species are shaped as they are. A glance at the eggs of a ground-nesting shorebird, such as the Grey (Black-bellied) Plover, shows that the four

| | |
|---|---|
| Meadow Pipit | Cuckoo |
| Sedge Warbler | Cuckoo |
| Wren | Cuckoo |
| Reed Bunting | Cuckoo |

### The Cuckoo

Female Cuckoos specialize in particular host nests when laying their eggs. Over generations they have evolved eggs that bear a close resemblance to those of the host.

## Uninvited guests

Among the world's birds, there are about 80 species that lay their eggs in the nests of other birds and leave incubation and rearing to foster parents. Yet though we tend to link such brood parasitism with the Cuckoos, only just over a third of the world's 125 Cuckoos actually behave in this way. In fact, none of the North American Cuckoos is brood parasitic, though there are other birds that have adopted the parasitic strategy. Foremost among these are the Cowbirds. The Brown-headed Cowbird has been recorded laying its eggs in the nests of over 200 different species though, like the Eurasian Cuckoo, it does have distinct preferences. The Cuckoo, veritable symbol of unfaithfulness, has laid its eggs in the nests of no less than 300 species, though it too specializes in a relatively few common species. In fact, female Cuckoos tend to specialize in a particular species and lay eggs that bear a strong resemblance to those of the host. It is an expert nest-finder and regularly lays up to 15 eggs in the nests of potential hosts.

**Below** Many ground nesting birds, like the European Woodcock, lay camouflaged eggs. When they hatch, the white interior of the shells spoils the effect, producing a moment of danger before the young move away.

eggs fit neatly together with points toward the centre like the segments of an orange. With birds that lay many more eggs than that number, the advantage of such a shape quickly disappears. The Guillemot (Common Murre) lays a single egg that is so sharply pointed it spins rather than rolls, a great advantage to a bird that lays its egg on a tiny ledge often high up a sheer cliff.

# INCUBATION AND REARING THE YOUNG

**Above** Like the other Plovers, the Lapwing lays well camouflaged eggs that merge well with the grassy fields preferred by these widely spread birds.

**Right** The burden of forming and incubating the clutch of eggs places a heavy strain on many birds. This male Robin feeds his mate partly to nourish her, but also to reinforce their bond.

The objective of a bird's nesting routine is to raise as many young as possible to independence. The choice of nest site and nest construction, the timing of breeding, the number, and colour and shape of the eggs and even the incubation routine are all geared to this end.

### Incubation routines

As with other aspects of birds' lives, incubation routines vary enormously from one species to another. Most species develop an incubation patch during the breeding season and, while mostly it is the females that have this patch of bare skin on their breasts and bellies, in some birds it is only the male and in others both sexes show this feature. The presence of a brood patch generally indicates the role of the sexes in incubation. In some species males may lack a brood patch and take no part in incubation at all, though they may or may not contribute to feeding and caring for the young. In other species, they may take an equal share, while in some, like the Phalaropes, the male may take sole charge of the chores of incubation and rearing the young. Such role-reversal, as it is

called, is a well developed tactic among many of the shorebirds that breed in the high Arctic where the season is so remarkably short. With the Phalaropes it is the female that is more boldly coloured, that takes the most active role in courtship and leaves her eggs in sole charge of the male. Meanwhile she is free to find another mate and produce another clutch of eggs, thus maximizing the chances of rearing young.

Some species, such as the Owls, start incubating as soon as the first egg is laid, but many others do not start until the clutch is complete. The latter routine, adopted by most ground-nesting birds as well as by many small birds, has the advantage that the young all hatch at more or less the same time. With ground-nesting birds such

as the shorebirds and Grouse, the young are active soon after hatching and can leave the nest in search of food and to avoid danger. If the young hatched over a period of a week or more, the adults would have the problem of guarding the active young while continuing with the incubation of the remaining eggs; clearly an impossible task. Most small birds hatch naked, blind and helpless and must be fed by their parents for two or three weeks in the safety of the nest. Synchronized hatching, that is all the eggs hatching within a few hours of one another, produces a brood of similarly sized young. With Owls, the eggs hatch over the same period of time that they were laid, producing a brood of different-sized youngsters. The eldest gets the lion's share of the food and is completely satisfied before the next largest and strongest is fed. This tactic means that if food is abundant the Owls will rear many young, but if it is short only the strongest will be fed and survive. The later hatched owlets will simply die of starvation. Though it is less obvious, small birds have a similar tactic. The adults feed the largest and most available mouth each time they visit the nest, rather than share the food equally among all their young.

This seems remarkably cruel and unfair, quite unlike the behaviour of a human parent. Yet it has the advantage that, when food is in short supply, at least one or two young will be reared, rather than the whole brood dying for lack of food.

### The strain of incubation

A great many birds share the chore of incubation so that each gets time off away from the nest to feed, drink and bathe. Nevertheless, despite the long days of summer, the process places an enormous strain on the adults. During the early part of incubation the sitting bird may leave the nest quickly and discreetly at the slightest sign of danger. The stimulus of danger is much more powerful than the drive to incubate. But, as the eggs get closer and closer to hatching, the drive to incubate grows in strength and the sitting bird becomes progressively more reluctant to leave the nest. At this time birds may appear remarkably tame, allowing a closer approach than at any other time of the year. Some Scandinavian waders have returned to incubate their eggs held in a human hand, even when the hand is lifted from the ground. An exceptional case occurred in Scotland when a Red Grouse was found burnt to death on her clutch of eggs after a moorland fire.

With most small birds incubation lasts about two weeks, but the young Eurasian Cuckoo hatches in 11 or 12 days, so that it is older than its siblings and can eject them, before or after hatching, and have the nest and its foster parents to itself - essential for so large and voracious a youngster. Other species have longer incubation periods, with most Eagles having to incubate their

**Left** After three weeks or more of incubation this young Oystercatcher has started to break out of its eggshell. The white spot on its bill is a special egg-tooth that is lost soon after hatching.

**Above** Laid on its back, a Marsh Tit will show the bare skin of its brood patch when a few loose feathers are lifted.

eggs for six or seven weeks. Longest periods of all are those of the larger Albatrosses which can last up to 10 or 11 weeks.

After a variable, but always lengthy, period of incubation the eggs hatch to produce young birds. They may vary from the naked, blind and helpless chicks of many typical garden birds, to the downy and camouflaged young of the shorebirds and Grouse. In both cases the behaviour of the parents undergoes a radical and rapid change. The stimulus system of eggs and incubation becomes young-brood, then begging mouth-feed.

Many young birds have remarkably colourful gapes (mouths), often spotted with contrasting colours. The response of the adult is to thrust food at the spots. It is a simple stimulus-response situation. Generally, the larger the mouth the more food is thrust into it, which, as we have seen, has the effect of satisfying the strongest and most

**Above** Young Woodpigeons are unable to digest the grain and seeds that form the diet of adults, so they are fed on "pigeon's milk" secreted from the lining of the parent's stomach.

**Left** Garden Warblers are summer visitors to Europe that time their arrival and breeding activities to coincide with the hatch of green caterpillars of the various winter moths.

advanced chick at the expense of its siblings. The work-rate of adults feeding a brood of hungry youngsters is often prodigious. Literally hundreds of sorties in search of food are flown every day in the effort to satisfy an ever-hungry brood.

### Hatching times

The timing of hatching is often critical in many species, particularly those that rear only a single brood each year. The European Blue Tit is a typical example. It lays some seven to 12 eggs over a period of, say, 12 days, incubates for 12 to 16 days

and then feeds its young on the green caterpillars of the winter moth. Should the birds get their timing wrong, and the flush of caterpillars not be available, there is little or no chance of their being able to rear a successful brood. Yet, despite the fact that the caterpillar hatch can vary in the time of its appearance from year to year, the Blue Tits get it right season after season. Just how they manage this is still a matter of conjecture.

The tactic of feeding the young at the nest is adopted by a huge number of different species and, in many cases, involves the adults in a remarkable change of diet. Many seed-eating Finches change to become insect-hunters, either during the entire summer or at least to feed their young. Species that cannot adapt to such a change are unusual, but do include the Pigeons and Doves, which feed their young on a liquid substance called pigeons' milk that is secreted from the lining of their crop. Clearly, this is a far more nutritious and more easily digestible diet than one of hard grain seeds.

### The young on the nest

Most birds carry food to their young in their bills and, during this phase of the breeding cycle, nests are particularly easy to locate. It is, therefore, a time for caution by the would-be nest watcher. A few species actually eat the food collected and return to the nest with empty bills. Young Cormorants are particularly adept at getting their parents to regurgitate partly digested food for them to eat and, late on in the rearing process, will actually thrust their bills and heads deep inside the adult's gullet to obtain the goods. The Pelicans have a similar process, though in their case the food is regurgitated into the adult's bill pouch, which acts as a sort of plate.

Eagles and other birds of prey carry food in their talons and arrive back at the nest with items that are quite beyond the chicks' ability to deal with. The adult will then tear tiny morsels from its catch to feed delicately to its young. As they grow in size, power and appetite, such tendernesses are abandoned and prey is simply dumped at the nest for the youngsters to feed themselves. Some quickly learn to tear up their own prey, but there is often an intermediate period during which quite large items may be swallowed whole. Young Owls have been timed taking up to an hour or more as they struggle to down a substantial rodent.

Many ground-nesting birds produce active young that quickly leave the nest and feed themselves. Mallard on the park pond are a good example, but Ducks, Geese and most shorebirds follow a similar routine. Some of these species, particularly the various species of diving Ducks, are hole-nesters and, utilizing old Woodpecker holes, the young may find themselves high above the ground. This is, however, no deterrence and at only a few hours of age the whole brood will throw themselves one after the other into the air to reach their encouraging parent below. They do, of course, bounce, but accidents are actually surprisingly rare.

Adults of species that produce self-feeding young still have to brood and warm their offspring as well as protect them from predators. Most of these species have a distinctive alarm call that elicits an instant and immobile crouching on the part of the chicks. They may scatter and crouch and rely on their camouflage to avoid becoming food to another species. Some, such as the Plovers, have evolved an elaborate injury-feigning display by the adults to draw the attention of the predator away from their young. Such distraction displays often involve what appears to be a broken wing dragged over the ground.

**Below** Mistle Thrushes breed early in the year, often before the trees have come into leaf. For this reason the nest is usually placed in the major low fork of a large tree.

# LIFESPANS

It is a reasonable assumption that the larger the potential number of young an individual species is capable of rearing, the shorter the lifespan the fledgling can expect. In other words, species that can replace and maintain their numbers by rearing only a single youngster a year must live longer than those that rear 10 or 12. It is also reasonably obvious that if we notice about the same number of individuals of a particular species year after year, but know that the species concerned lays, say, two clutches of five eggs each, then an awful lot of eggs, chicks and fledglings cannot have survived their first year.

**The survival of the fittest**
In fact, most small birds do not survive to breed at all; but the longer they survive the longer still they are likely to live. The most vulnerable part of a bird's life is in the nest, for whole clutches of eggs are lost to predators, bad weather and accidents: and as a nestling the youngster faces the same

**Left** Many ground nesting birds, like this Little Ringed Plover, perform elaborate displays of injury feigning to draw would-be predators away from their eggs or young.

**Above** The young of this Willow Warbler were born naked, blind and helpless. Within three weeks they will fend for themselves and soon after set out on a migratory flight across the Sahara Desert.

threats and is equally vulnerable. Eventually, it fledges, leaves the nest on poorly developed wings and is quite incapable of feeding and fending for itself. The death of a parent at this, and any earlier stage, can be a disaster.

Having become independent, the young bird has to learn the ways of the world, perfect its skills and build on the inherited knowledge with which it was born. Many will die before they acquire such skills and, in the case of migratory species, many more during their first long journey. Resident species will have to find sufficient food to see

them through the winter, for it is the leanest time of the year that causes the death of most adult birds. With small birds, those that survive will breed in their first year, but with larger birds adolescence may last two, three or even seven or eight years.

This period of immaturity is often spent well away from the breeding area, usually in the wintering area. Ospreys, for example, spend their first winter in the area where they will winter as adults. They may stay on for the subsequent summer and a second winter, but many will move northwards during their first spring and over-summer in between the breeding and wintering grounds. During their second summer they may move even further northwards and actually visit, but not breed in, their eventual summer homes. Such a gentle upbringing through adolescence may be an essential ingredient in their eventual success as breeding adults.

The larger Albatrosses of the southern hemisphere enjoy a considerably longer period of immaturity. A youthful Royal Albatross cannot expect to breed until it is eight years old and may not even do so until its 11th year. This extended period is probably necessary to enable the bird to become expert at finding its food and dealing with the vagaries of the southern storm belt. The young Albatross will circle the world over and over again during this adolescence. Even when fully mature the great Albatrosses breed only in alternate years, so long is the period of nesting, incubation and care of the young. Clearly, such birds can expect to reach a ripe old age, perhaps as long as man. We certainly have records of one Royal Albatross that was ringed when at least eight or nine years old in 1937 and was still breeding in New Zealand in 1988 at over 60 years of age.

### Life expectations

For most birds, however, life is short. The average mature individual - that is a bird that has survived all the dangers of being reared and successfully fledged - may still enjoy a life expectancy of a year or less. The mature American Robin and European Song Thrush can expect to live a further 11 months, a Starling 18 months, a Woodcock over two years and a Swift over three years. Most deaths are the result of accident or predation, for very few birds die of old age whilst in the wild.

The influence of man on a bird's life may be particularly important, and most game birds live relatively short lives. The average adult Mallard cannot expect to live another year and most Grouse share that fate. Generally, these birds produce large clutches of eggs and have the ability to make speedy recoveries from population crashes. The ban on shooting Brent Geese in some areas has resulted in an enormous increase in the numbers of these high-Arctic breeders, showing that the previous decline was largely due to conditions on their wintering grounds.

Species that reproduce only slowly, such as the Albatrosses and most larger birds of prey, cannot compensate for persecution and may take many years to recover their numbers.

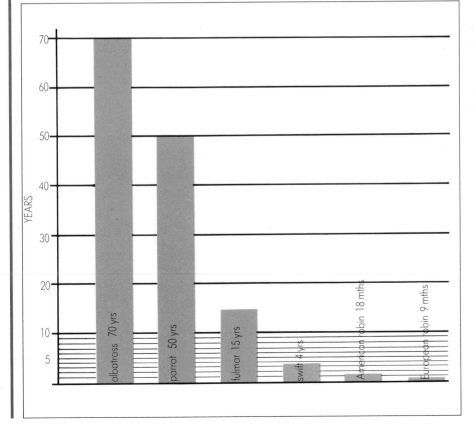

**Left** The average lifespan of various species is correlated with the age at which they breed; the number of eggs laid; and the number of young reared. Many small birds do not survive their first year.

# LOOKING OUTWARDS: BINOCULARS

Knowing the birds that live alongside us, that share our home, or at least our garden, and understanding something of the ways in which birds live, we are now ready to start looking outwards to the birds that live beyond the garden fence. Some species will never alight in our gardens, even if they sometimes fly over, and it is part of the natural progression to becoming an ornithologist or birder to want to see new birds. At first the local park may produce a few new birds, particularly if it offers habitats, such as a pond, that do not exist in the garden. Then we may hear of a nearby woodland, marsh, estuary or, if we are lucky, a nearby bird reserve. Visits at any time of the year will start producing new birds, birds that we have previously seen only illustrated in books or magazines. But just as we expect to see different birds in the garden at different seasons, so can we expect different birds to appear in these other habitats on a seasonal basis. Some people become so involved in their garden that they seldom venture much further and satisfy

**Above** A group of birders on the Isles of Scilly, England, with every pair of binoculars focused on some poor transatlantic waif. The total value of the optical gear brought to bear amounts to tens of thousands of pounds.

themselves by producing even better bird conditions in their own back yard. Others find a particularly satisfying habitat or area near their homes and become dedicated to their "local patch". Most of us enjoy both of these types of birding, yet still wish to travel progressively further afield in search of more and more birds.

### Binoculars – a birding essential .

It was often said (and written) in the past that watching birds was one of the cheapest of all hobbies. It required no equipment, just an inquiring mind. This is (and was) rubbish. Watching birds requires at the very least a pair of binoculars - or field glasses as they were previously called. To try to enjoy birding without optical aid is to doom oneself to endless frustration.

There are, however, binoculars and binoculars; a pair of opera glasses or a monocular just will not do. Neither will a pair of glasses inherited from a distant and aged relative. Good binoculars have never been as freely available as they are today, but the beginner should beware and seek expert advice from other birders or a book (which is what

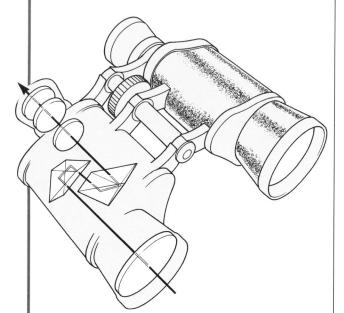

**Above** A section through a pair of modern prismatic binoculars shows the passage of light via two multi-faced prisms and thence via magnifying and focusing lenses to the eye.

you, dear reader, are doing right now).

Birders have several major requirements in a binocular that are different from those of other users. Coastguards need powerful magnifications so that they can identify individual ships at great distances by reading their names or numbers. They also need binoculars that will function in poor light. Such a combination leads them to choose huge binoculars mounted on a stand or tripod, after all they do not have to carry them around. Seafarers have similar requirements, but do not enjoy the stability of a land-based watch point. They thus choose less magnification and a lighter, easier-to-keep-steady binocular that is also robust and waterproof. Horse-racing enthusiasts need binoculars similar to those required by bird-watchers, though they are generally naive about optics and settle for an over-large pair with a case slung low on the hip like a gun-holster.

## What magnification

So birders have to make a compromise between magnification, light-gathering power, field of view and weight. No one wants to carry an albatross around their neck all day and heavy weights are very difficult to hold steady in use. A magnification between seven or 10 times is perfect for birding and should be chosen by all. The field of view and light gathering power of a binocular depend on the size of the object lens - that's the big one at the front. By convention these lenses are described by their measured diameter in millimetres, for example 25, 30, 40 or 50. A full description of the specification of a pair of binoculars is expressed as the magnification (say 10) times (x) the diameter of the object lens (say 40).

The basic description is, however, only the start, for binoculars vary enormously in weight, field of view, sharpness, twilight power and so on. Modern "roof prism" binoculars have no external moving parts and are also relatively dust-proof and damp-resistant. They have a central focusing knob and a variable adjustment on one eyepiece that enables the individual to compensate for differences between the eyes. Some makes are expensive, some relatively cheap; frankly you get what you pay for. If there is any chance of your becoming a keen birder buy the best you can afford in the range 8 to 10 magnification and 35 to 50 diameter object lens.

**Right** Though binoculars are the essential everyday tool of bird watchers throughout the world, there are a few sites, such as this colony of Sooty Terns, where they may actually be a hindrance.

# TELESCOPES AND TRIPODS

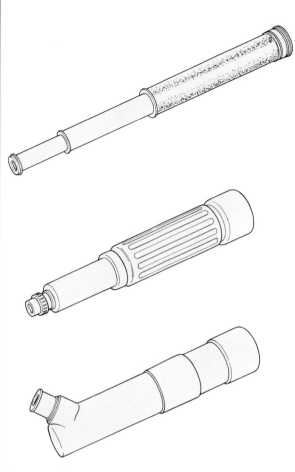

Three quite different telescopes show the range of instruments now available. **Top** An old fashioned, multiple-draw 'scope that is focused by pushing and pulling. **Middle** A modern single-draw 'scope focused by turning the eye-piece.
**Bottom** A prismatic 'scope is much shorter and therefore much easier to handle.

Armed with a decent pair of binoculars one can watch birds anywhere in the world, but it soon becomes obvious that many birds can be picked out, but not identified, at greater distances. Today more and more birders are making use of telescopes which can be clamped to a car window or a hide (blind), or mounted on a tripod. Interestingly, most of these instruments were designed for use by target shooters, but manufacturers are at last getting round to the idea that bird-watchers are a distinct market with their own criteria of judgement.

## Lenses and magnification

Not so long ago telescopes were left-overs from a military era and were heavy, multi-draw, brass contraptions better suited to the battlefields of the First World War than the modern, high-speed campaign favoured by contemporary birders.

**Below** The telescope and tripod combination is becoming a standard piece of birding equipment, especially when watching birds along shorelines and other open areas.

**Right** Though the telescope and tripod are heavy and cumbersome to carry, they have an immense advantage over the hand-held telescope in use.

Today's optics are light, easy to use and highly efficient. Magnifications vary from about x20 to x40 and beyond and there are lenses that will zoom through a huge range of magnifications. These zoom 'scopes would seem to be perfect for birding, but nothing is for free. The very structure of a zoom lens means that one loses on the field of view, making it less easy to pick out a particular bird. In fact, most zooms can "see" about 60 to 70 percent of the area that can be seen with a fixed magnification of the same power. For most purposes a magnification of x20 to x25 is perfectly satisfactory - though it is a good idea to choose a 'scope on which the eyepieces (that is the magnification) can easily be interchanged. The addition of a x30 or x35 eyepiece may just come in handy on the odd occasion.

As with binoculars, the other half of the equation is the diameter of the object lens measured in millimetres. The larger the diameter the more light is gathered, but the heavier the 'scope. The usual compromise is between a 50mm and 70mm object lens, with a tendency towards the larger diameters with new lightweight glass. So far no company has produced a 'scope using the even larger diameter lenses used by modern sports photographers, though several companies

are heading in the right direction.

At time of writing the "draw" telescope is on the wane and even single draw 'scopes are probably doomed to extinction. The 'scope of the moment and, dare I say the future, is a prismatic with no moving external parts. Several well-established firms dominate this market producing ever better instruments in competition one with another. As ever, you pay for what you get.

### The prismatic scope

Settling then on a modern prismatic 'scope with a x20 to x25 fixed magnification and a 60mm or 70mm object lens the choice remains between a "straight-through" or "angled" eyepiece. For many years I have been a confirmed devotee of the latter. Angled eyepieces have several major advantages. Firstly, they can comfortably be used on lower tripods. This means that they suffer less buffeting in the wind and, more important then this, I can "pass" a bird to a companion through the 'scope without having to lower (or raise) the height of the instrument. The latter is important if, like me, you spend much of your time showing birds to others. Secondly, it is much easier to watch a bird higher than oneself, such as a bird of prey in the air. Frankly, the only disadvantage is that it may be more difficult to locate a particular bird with an angled eye-piece, though I have never found this a problem myself and it may be only the opinion of those who have never used the "angled" job on a regular basis.

Naked eye

8 × binoculars

20 × telescope

**Magnification**

The effect of using modern binoculars (× 8 magnification) and a telescope (× 20 magnification). Note that although the bird appears closer the greater the magnification used, the field of view decreases dramatically making the bird progressively more difficult to find.

# THE COMPLETE BIRDER

Armed with a good pair of binoculars one can watch birds anywhere in the world. Add a telescope and it is reasonable to imagine that one is prepared for birding at all seasons. There has, however, been something of a revolution in birding equipment over the past 20 or so years, so that the modern enthusiast often has as much equipment as the dedicated coarse fisherman.

The equipment boom can be divided into a number of categories the most significant of which is optical gear. To add a second pair of binoculars to one's armoury seems sensible. Even the most expensive glasses can break down and cause missed opportunities. A spare, higher powered pair of binoculars also can be very useful, for example on long sea-watches. A magnification of x15 or even x20 may be impossible to carry round the neck all day, but is marvellous for watching autumn Skuas.

**The advantages of a tripod**
Telescopes have a great versatility, particularly when mounted on a tripod. Indeed this combination is now the second favourite piece of equipment after binoculars. For preference the tripod should be as light as possible, but also as sturdy and firm as possible. This contradiction leads inevitably to yet another compromise: the best telescope support is immovable, yet mobility is of the essence. Several makes are favoured by birders, but an easy action and light weight are features that should govern the choice.

Telescope-tripod combinations are awkward to carry about and shoulder straps are essential. These can be attached to the tripod by using the large split rings designed to hold keys. The broader the strap the more comfortable the contraption is to carry. Before leaving telescopes it is worth mentioning again the interchangeable eyepieces that are available for several of the better known and more favoured makes. Most birders prefer x20 to x25 fixed magnifications and many carry a spare, say x30 to x35, for those occasions when a little more power can convert a "probable" into a "definite" species. Personally, I don't; but I am quite happy to borrow a 'scope from someone else who is prepared to lug around a lot of of extra gear.

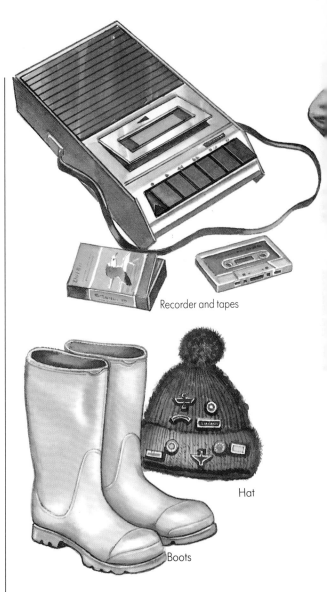

Recorder and tapes

Hat

Boots

Protecting one's optical equipment against accidental damage seems sensible, but is generally approached in a somewhat cavalier fashion by most birders. To be seen with a manufacturer's carrying case over the shoulder is positively out! Whereas to have a rain guard that slips up and down the binocular strap is definitely in! However, this should slip up and down one strap, not two as the designer intended! Telescopes are generally better treated and many birders bind them with protective tape to prevent chipping of the enamel. Some Scandinavian birders cover their 'scopes with expanded polystyrene creating a huge white sausage with holes for the working parts. This may be going a little too far, but it is a good idea to bind

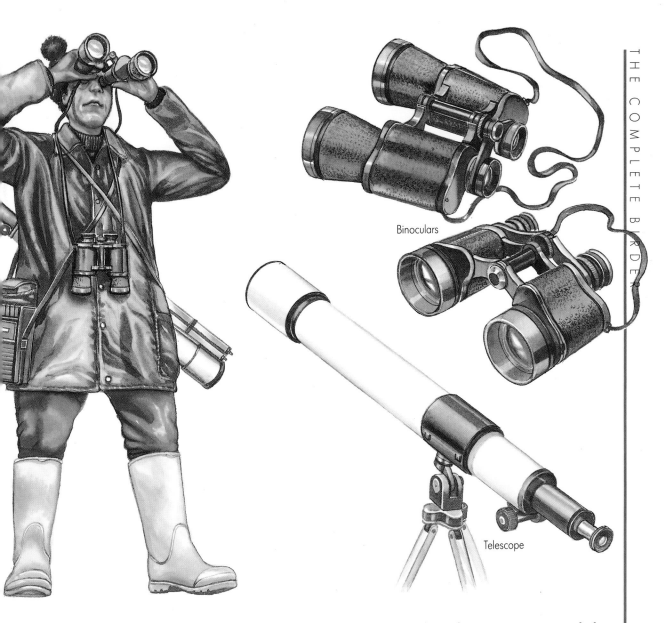

Binoculars

Telescope

any joints through which water could enter the optical system.

**Clothing**

The "one-upmanship" of birding (birdmanship) depends largely on a set of visual signals. These are all designed to show that one is a "real" birder, who travels the world, sees rare birds virtually daily and, above all, spends long hours "in the field". Binoculars must therefore, look used not new. Telescopes should be taped, though the tape should be worn. Barbour jackets may be worn by other countryside users and even by city trendies, but birders ensure that theirs are well worn and in need of repair. Bruce Campbell, the well-known writer and birdwatcher, once suggested that throwing a new jacket into a chicken run was the best method of "distressing", but contemporary chickens seldom have such freedom.

Waterproof boots, "wellies", may be essential, but are not conducive to lengthy walking. Most birders, of all ages, prefer trainers which are light, comfortable and decidedly not waterproof.

Birders today use tape recorders, cassettes of bird songs, a variety of distressed clothing for various weather situations, as well as tripods, telescopes, interchangeable eyepieces and binoculars. They also tend to sport woolly hats, usually covered with "bird" badges, and cars similarly adorned with "bird" stickers.

# IDENTIFICATION

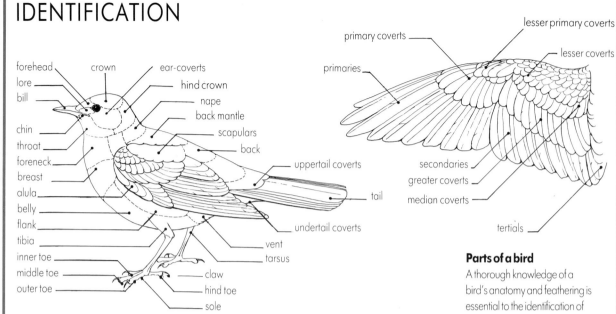

forehead
crown
ear-coverts
lore
hind crown
bill
nape
back mantle
chin
scapulars
throat
back
foreneck
breast
alula
belly
flank
tibia
inner toe
tarsus
middle toe
claw
outer toe
hind toe
sole

uppertail coverts

undertail coverts

vent

tail

primary coverts
lesser primary coverts
primaries
lesser coverts

secondaries
greater coverts
median coverts

tertials

**Parts of a bird**
A thorough knowledge of a
bird's anatomy and feathering is
essential to the identification of
many species.

**Above** Small shorebirds
pose identification problems of
the highest order, particularly

when, like this Little Stint, they are
in nondescript winter plumage.

The primary skill of birding is being able to put a
name to every bird seen, even with the briefest
and most distant of views, and many highly skilled
watchers never get beyond this fascinating aspect
of birds. As a result, the art of identification is
continually progressing. Not so long ago several
species were written up in field guides as "not
separable" in the field - today's birders have
responded to the challenge.

### Identification points

Though most identification books tend to
concentrate on the colour of birds, with
abbreviated plumage descriptions, most good
birders have a sound knowledge of structure to act
as a basis of identification. In fact, even beginners
have an elementary knowledge of structure and
virtually anyone can identify a Duck as a Duck, a
Wader as a Wader, a Hawk as a Hawk and so on.
Learning the characteristics of other groups;
picking out a Warbler as a Warbler, or a Bunting, a
Chat, a Pipit, a Diver or a Grebe as such, is not
difficult and such distinctions are largely a matter
of structure.

Other structural features may be a little more
elusive, but still provide the most important clues
to a bird's identity. The shape of the wings can be
particularly useful. Are they long and narrow like a
Swift's? Are they short and rounded like a
Grouse's? Are the wings broad and square like a
Vulture's? Or are they rounded like a
Sparrowhawk's? Are they sharply angled like a
Swallow's? Or are they straight like a Shearwater's?
With all birds wing shape is important, but with
birds of prey shape may be the most significant
feature of all. Many such birds are uniformly dark
brown and identification relies entirely on
structure.

Tail shape too can be vitally important. Some

birds have long pointed tails like Pintail and Long-tailed Skuas. Others have deeply forked tails like the Barn Swallow. All other birds fit somewhere into this spectrum of tail shape with wedge-shaped, rounded, square or notched tails. But shape and length are not the same and the proportionate length of a bird's tail may be one of its most significant field marks.

Similarly, not only do the shape and structure of a bird's bill tell us much about its lifestyle, but they can also prove an invaluable aid to identification. Swallows have tiny bills, but huge mouths. Grosbeaks, as their name implies, have huge, crunching bills. Hawks have distinctly hooked bills, but then so have Parrots. Curlews have long decurved bills, whereas Snipe have long, straight ones. Length of bill may be difficult for the beginner to express, for terms like "long" and "very long" are more or less meaningless. So birders compare the length of a bird's bill to the distance between the eye and the base of the bill (the loral distance) or, for really long bills, to the length of the head through the eye. We say, for example, that a European Robin has a bill about the same length as the loral distance, and that a Godwit has a bill about 21/2 times the length of the head. Similarly, the length of tail can, in flying and particularly soaring birds, be compared with the width of the wing. In many Eagles these are about equal, though a slightly longer tail can change one species of Eagle into another. A Harrier, on the other hand, has a tail that is almost twice as long as the width of the wing.

Size, too, can be a very useful identification tool, though it should be approached with great caution. An unknown bird should always be compared with that of a species that is well known and we say that a bird is "Sparrow-sized", "Starling-sized" and so on. Better still is to relate a bird with a known species with which it keeps company and can be directly compared. Even here, however, one should be careful of the effect of binoculars, which can make a bird further away appear larger than a closer bird. If you find this hard to believe, try looking through binoculars along a railway line and see how the parallel lines appear to diverge rather than come together in true perspective - but don't take too long in making this test!

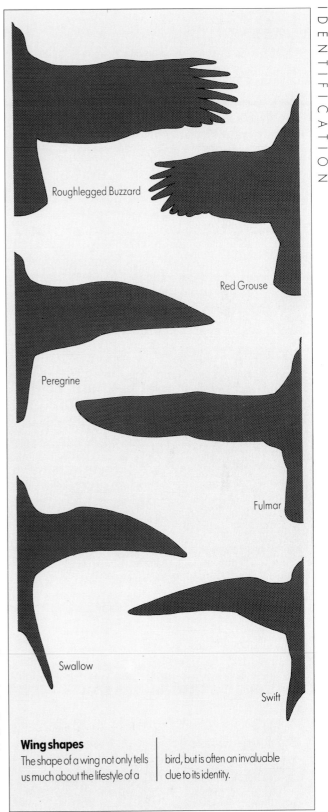

Roughlegged Buzzard

Red Grouse

Peregrine

Fulmar

Swallow

Swift

**Wing shapes**
The shape of a wing not only tells us much about the lifestyle of a bird, but is often an invaluable clue to its identity.

# FIELD GUIDES

The main aid to identification, even in an increasingly technological age, is the field guide, a book that illustrates and describes all the different birds one is ever likely to see in a particular area or region. Even 30 years ago, colour printing was something of a novelty: today we take it for granted and it is unthinkable that a modern field guide would not be illustrated in colour throughout. This facility means that everything we need to name a bird can be grouped together rather than scattered somewhat randomly over several pages. Colour printing is, however, still expensive and inevitably the publishers of any field guide have to make a choice between producing an expensive book that deals in depth with a small area for a small market, or a cheap one covering a much larger area and for a correspondingly larger market. In Europe this tends to mean that field guides cover the whole of the continent rather than just an individual country. In America they cover the whole country, rather than any individual state. Only by printing tens of thousands can the high cost of colour illustration be amortized to produce a cheap book.

## What to look for

The essential ingredients of any field guide are colour illustrations of the bird; a descriptive text that complements rather than repeats information supplied by the illustration; and maps showing where the bird is found. A good field guide will, additionally, illustrate every major plumage of every bird, including sex and age differences as well as illustrating both the upper and under surfaces of the bird in flight if that is how they are often seen. The text will describe each of these plumages, as well as picking out where and when the bird is found, together with some idea of its abundance and "visibility". The maps will show not only where a bird is found in summer when it is breeding, but also where it winters and areas that it passes through on migration.

As we enter the 1990s, there is a wide range of field guides available which, to a varying extent, meet these criteria. They cover various parts of the world, though inevitably the widest choice covers those areas - Europe and North America - that have the highest populations of birdwatchers.

These areas have several excellent field guides from which to choose and, although we all have our favourites, there is a great deal to be said for having several in the field. In Europe the guides by Peterson, Mountfort and Hollom; by Heinzel and Fitter; by Bruun and Singer; and (dare I say) Gooders and Harris (1990) are all worth having. In North America, one should have the Peterson; the Golden Guide; and the National Geographic Guide.

Elsewhere in the world, field guides vary from the excellent to the pathetic, with some countries being well served and others without a single book to aid the traveller. Visiting even well-known bird areas such as East Africa, India or parts of South

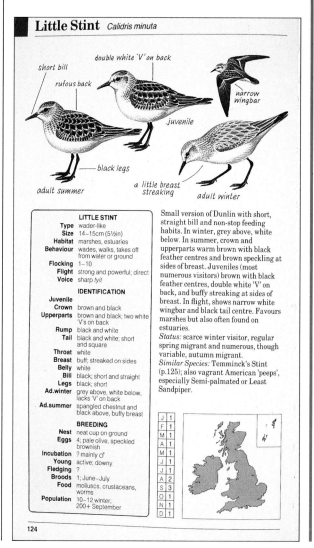

**Left** This guide shows each bird in both summer and winter plumage, as well as in flight, making it easier to make a correct identification. (Courtesy Kingfisher Books)

**Above** A good field guide is essential for anyone interested in birds. There is a vast selection available, ranging from those which cover specific areas to the more general.

America can, therefore, be a very frustrating experience. The main problem is the cost of completeness, for with an avifauna of anything over 500 species the expense involved in producing a full-colour guide cannot be recouped from sales to visitors alone.

One of my colleagues has overcome the problem by buying two copies of every field guide available for anywhere in the world, plus two copies of any other well-illustrated bird book. He then sets to cutting out the individual birds and pasting them into scrap books for his journeys. This may work out expensive, and frankly I personally cannot bring myself to cut up books! Nevertheless, it is one answer to the problem. There are, however, more and more guides,

covering wider and wider areas, so that by early next century book maltreatment in Boston may be a thing of the past. By then, however, we may have adopted a completely new technology, based on the computer or the video disc.

Field guides are not only essential for identifying birds in the field, they are also excellent bedside books. When beginning birds, or when planning a trip to a new area or region, taking the field guide to bed and poring over the possibilities is a splendid way of getting to know the birds that will be new to you. Slowly but surely, you get to know what to look for in an individual species and, most importantly, you find out in advance the often subtle differences between closely allied and similar species. Anyone, for instance, intending to visit Africa should work thoroughly through the various species of Weaver. Many are golden with black heads in the male and only by knowing the minor distinctions will most of these birds be identified. Anyway, as field guides lack any sense of plot, they are generally better at sending one to sleep than spy stories.

# FIELD NOTEBOOK

Opinion is divided as to whether or not one should carry a field guide in the field and whether one should consult it when faced with an unidentified bird. In general it is thought that with the bird before one, it is likely that the book will suggest identification features that you will then manage to find, thus hoodwinking you into seeing what you want to see rather than what is actually there. Purists, therefore, feel that taking a good set of field notes should precede book consultation. Despite these opinions, books are much in evidence whenever a rare bird is being observed and, for the beginner, every new bird is a "rarity".

Writing a description of an unknown bird requires practice and it is surely better to practise and perfect the technique in advance than to wait for a rarity to turn up and then find that you lack the skill to describe it. Even a humble garden bird makes a perfect subject for a field description.

## Compiling a description

The description should start with the circumstances. Where and when was the bird seen, what was it doing, what other birds were associating with it, what size was it and what were your overall impressions? Next describe, part by part, the upperparts of the bird, starting at the forehead and progressing via crown, nape, mantle, wings and rump to the tail. Follow with a similar

**Below** Identifying ducks in flight depends on picking out the salient features, often marks on the upper wing. Knowing what to look for on each species is essential.

**Above** A page from a field notebook shows the value of drawings in noting the salient points on a bird seen flying over open land in midsummer.

**Left and below** Drawing birds may be an art, but the use of ovals to create the basic shape is crucial to the beginner and professional alike.

**Above left** The Spotted Flycatcher is a small brown bird, virtually devoid of field marks. It does, however, have the characteristic habit of flying out from a prominent perch, catching a fly and returning to the same place.

**Above** Correctly identifying American Flycatchers is often a matter of making careful field notes and checking the crucial points with handbooks. This Great Crested Flycatcher can be confused with three other very similar species.

description of the underparts from chin, throat, neck, breast, belly to undertail. Learn the names of the different feather groups, especially those of the wing both when folded and when spread, and use the names in your description. Next describe the bill and legs, for some reason often called the bird's "soft parts"! Finally if, while identifying the bird, you considered other species, put them down together with the reasons you had for eliminating them. At the end state, in percentage terms, how sure you are of the identification. You may care to make a rough drawing of the bird, using arrows and notes to pick out the diagnostic points, and many birders make such sketches as a form of shorthand prior to a detailed description. At first, these drawings will be pretty crude, but it is surprising how quickly one can progress. Remember that birds are just two ovals joined together in varying relationships.

**Permanent records**

The other major use of a field notebook is to keep a record of what you have seen. In some cases this is no more than a list of birds together with the number of individuals.

For most of us, though, the field notebook is neither more nor less than is implied in the name: a place to record what we see and when we see it. My own notebooks are full of the most obscure information, varying from a whole page on, say, the wing angles of soaring and hovering Rough-legged Buzzards, to names and addresses of people I meet, and access details for sites that I may seldom visit.

At the end of the year, it is a great pleasure to thumb through the pages as a sort of vicarious reliving of the birding experiences enjoyed. It is also a good time to pick out the significant from the mundane and write up the records for the local county or state bird report.

# PHOTOGRAPHY

Photographing birds is worth a book in its own right and many have been written over the years. Most are full of good advice, describe the various techniques and equipment, and are written by experts. However, in my own mind at least, I divide bird photographers into two distinct types: there are birdwatchers who take up photography, and photographers who choose birds as a subject. By and large the work of the latter is superior to that of the former.

Photography is an art form and great photographs are taken with care, thought and an artistic eye. Most professional photographers employ an assistant who, apart from a variety of different functions, actually releases the shutter to expose the film. Bird photography does not quite fit such a process, though the nearer it comes to doing so the better the finished result.

The first thing to do if you want to photograph birds is to decide to what use the finished results

are to be put. In its simplest terms this may involve a choice between film for producing prints to illustrate a diary, or film to produce a slide show for your friends or a local bird-watching group. You may, however, harbour dreams of selling your work; if so then great care must be chosen in selecting the right film. All colour photographs that appear in magazines and books are taken from transparencies (slides). They are chosen by professional editors and designers not only on the basis of content, but also on technical merit. As a general rule, a slow, high-resolution, low-grain film produces a transparency that will reproduce in print much, much better than a faster film. So the film choice is limited and many transparencies

**Below** Photographing small, fast moving birds in dark woodland conditions poses a problem because of the reduced light available. Many photographers overcome this by using an electronic flash. This hide is set at a Pied Flycatcher's nest.

on fast film with huge lenses. Most use 35mm SLR cameras with lenses varying from 300mm to 1000mm in focal length. They use motor drives, automatic exposure systems and, sometimes, self-focusing devices. They take birds in bushes, on mud-flats and along the shoreline, both flying and standing still. Many of these action shots are obtained by stalking birds, using a shoulder holster for steadiness.

Others are more careful and more traditional. They set up hides at nests so that they can work closer to the birds and spend hours in preparation to obtain the perfect portrait. There is, however, a definite move away from nest photography and

**Above** To reach the nest of these Golden Orioles a tower hide was needed, and the photographer was rewarded with this delightful portrait of the pair together with their young.

**Right** Hides often need to be raised from the ground so that tree nesting birds can be satisfactorily photographed. Not all are as conveniently situated as this Mistle Thrush nest.

must be discarded because of out-of-focus subjects, or subjects that move. Modern, fast colour films that can be up-rated may produce lovely slides to show your friends, but they will not stand up to the test of reproduction.

**Camera selection**
Choice of film is then the first crucial element and its importance cannot be overstated. After that, all you need is a camera and you are into bird photography. Surprisingly, the modern single-lens reflex camera using 35mm film is used by both amateurs and professionals alike. These cameras are the most popular and widely available and are within the reach of even the shallowest of pockets. The only real essential for bird photography is the facility to change lenses.

To many, the idea of bird photography immediately conjures up a vision of huge telephoto lenses, but just as one should always use the slowest film possible, so too should one use the shortest lens that will do the job. With many small birds this will nevertheless be a telephoto of say 135mm, but the secret is to get closer to the subject rather than use a greater magnification.

Having put the, dare I say, professional standpoint, it is reassuring to know that there are hosts of people taking splendid bird photographs

towards using the same "controlled" techniques on other aspects of bird's lives. Birds come to feed and to drink in much the same way as they come to their nests and these activities offer varied and interesting opportunities for photography.

There is, I am pleased to say, also a more careful and artistic element entering into bird photography. Birds are now being photographed in their habitats, showing them more as we see them while birding. Over and over again such photographs are being chosen as winners in competitions, so that expensive and complex electronic equipment is taking second place to the eye of the photographer. To anyone starting out in the art, this is the most encouraging sign of all.

# RECORDING

The modern, portable tape recorder has revolutionized our approach to bird songs and calls. Thirty or so years ago, recordings were cut directly on to discs and the word "mobile" was used to indicate that a caravan, linked to a mains electricity supply, could be used as a transportable studio. Tape recorders changed that and modern cassette recorders have made it even easier to get out and about recording the sounds of birds wherever they can be heard.

The art of making recordings of bird song centres on isolating what has to be recorded from the general background of other noise. It is not sufficient to seek a quiet spot away from traffic, turn on the recorder and tape what can be heard. The result will be a quite unacceptable cacophony

**Left** Wildlife film maker Liz Bomford uses a parabolic reflector to obtain the required quality of sound for her television documentaries.

**Above** Portable tape recorders, combined with a parabolic reflector to focus the sound of a singing bird, enable even flying birds to be recorded.

of mixed-up sounds. Wind, even light wind, is the major enemy, but even on a still summer's morning miles away from roads, farmyards, chain saws and aircraft there is just too much noise in the countryside.

**Microphones and reflectors**
Isolation of the individual call requires a directional microphone similar to that used by

outside broadcasters and film makers. Mostly these professionals use a sausage-shaped object, often covered with fur and resembling a shaggy dog. This "sausage" contains a microphone and picks up sound mainly from the direction in which it is pointed. It is a robust, easy to handle form of directional microphone. It does, however, function best at close range. The alternative, and the solution chosen by most bird song recordists, is the parabolic reflector. This is a circular dish that concentrates the sound from a relatively narrow field to a single focus where the microphone is located. It thus works in the same way as a television dish for receiving signals from satellites.

Parabolic reflectors do not need to be huge and heavy and are available commercially at a reasonable price from several specialist manufacturers. Armed with one and a good quality cassette or tape recorder, anyone can record the songs and calls of birds in the wild.

Some recordists simply wander through likely spots recording as they go. Others treat recording as they would photography, and make elaborate preparations to record the particular species selected. This may involve placing the reflector close to a well-used song post with a lead to the recorder set up some distance away. In general, the longer the lead the less quality is obtained in the recording; so some recordists use hides just like photographers to obtain a really close approach. A few purists actually prefer to abandon the reflector and obtain a more "natural" recording by placing their microphone right at the bird's song post.

## Playing a recording

As with photography, there are several books available on making recordings of wildlife sounds, but for most of us the tape recorder serves quite a different purpose. Even a cheap cassette recorder with a built-in microphone will pick up a bird singing at relatively close range. If the recording is then played back to the bird, individuals of many species will approach to investigate, thus giving us an opportunity to view them openly and at close range. There are also commercially available recordings offering a huge range of bird songs and calls that can be played with similar effect. Calling birds up, in this way, can produce views of skulking birds and help to locate birds that have not been seen (or heard) at all. But using recordings in this way is not without its dangers.

Most birds that react to recordings will be on their breeding grounds, defending a territory. Investigating intruders and singing to defend their domains is a full-time job without having to contend with a human, apparently with a competitor sitting in his hands. A quick play and a satisfactory response probably does no harm, but a lengthy intrusion and particularly repeated intrusions may well interfere with the bird's breeding activities. So, as ever, moderation and thought for the bird are the key. Some ornithologists and conservationists believe that one should never play recordings to birds on territory - certainly rare birds should never be disturbed.

**Right** A casual, rather opportunistic approach to recording bird songs can be enjoyed by anyone, even on an ordinary walk through woodland.

# LISTING AND TICKING

**Right** A typical gathering of twitchers on the Isles of Scilly, England, in autumn. Similar, if smaller, groups of listers can be found on the island of Attu, the farthest west of the Aleutian Islands, Alaska.

When we start birding new birds come thick and fast and most of us, quite naturally, keep a list of all of the different birds we see. Gradually, new birds become harder to get; though conversely the thrill of seeing one increases. After a relatively short time the new bird for our list becomes exceptional and we may lose our interest in "listing" altogether. We may become interested in ringing (banding) or in the study of some relatively common species. We may start to travel further afield in our searches for new birds, or we may become twitchers (listers). Twitchers are birders who are prepared to travel various distances to see a particular bird that someone else has found. As we all like seeing a new bird and as most of us are prepared to travel a few miles to see it, I suppose we are all twitchers. It is, however, more accurate to reserve the term for those whose main activity is the search for rare birds throughout the year - even if they are birds that are discovered by someone else. Twitchers are geographically bound, for the new bird must be seen in the home county, state or country. As American twitchers are called "listers", the term properly refers only to British rarity hunters, whose main objective is to add new birds to their British list.

Twitching and listing have, by their critics, been likened to train-spotting, even though the skills and knowledge of twitchers are at a completely different level. These are dedicated and passionate people who, like every other close-knit group of enthusiasts, have developed their own code of conduct, their own standards and even their own language. They are thus a breed apart, but they should not be condemned for that.

**Phone-in system**
In many ways American listers have shown the way, for while British twitchers for long relied on an unofficial grapevine and messages relayed via an obscure Norfolk cafe, Americans were organized via a national phone-in system. That there is now a similar system in Britain (Birdcall - 0898 700227) is not surprising. The surprise is that it took so long to arrive. Inevitably, the arrival of a major rarity, one that has never - or only very seldom - been seen in the country before, will attract a large number of twitchers. The speed of modern communications may well produce a crowd of quite significant proportions and, if conditions are not conducive to mass access, there may be a need for crowd control and even

police assistance. Today most bird reserves welcome the arrival of a rarity, for twitchers are generally quite generous when they have seen a new bird and contribute to the reserve's funds. Access to private land can cause problems, but there are often "whip-rounds" to thank helpful landowners.

All twitchers keep a life list of the birds they have seen and most also a year list of birds seen each year. There is, of course, considerable competition for the best list on a year and life basis, but there are also continent and world listers. Some of the latter have seen well over half the birds in the world.

As a result of their enthusiasm and dedication, twitchers and listers build up a remarkable level of experience with the unusual birds they seek. Their level of identification skill is often quite exceptional and their conversation is liberally laced with references to obscure birds that most watchers only dream about.

The best advice to the would-be twitcher is to go for every rarity, meet people, talk to them and see if the enthusiasm rubs off. Like plumbing, it's an activity that's best learned on the job.

**Left** Ross's Gulls from the high Arctic pack ice occasionally stray southwards to send twitchers and listers alike into a frenzy of hurriedly cancelled appointments and mysteriously contracted minor illnesses.

**Below** A migrant Melodious Warbler in Britain often draws sizable groups of birders to ponder its identification, particularly the problem of distinguishing it from the similarly featureless Icterine Warbler.

# THE BIRDER'S YEAR

Understanding the main ingredients of the birds' year is essential if one is to get the best out of one's birding.

There is much to be said for getting to grips with the common residents before attempting the summer visitors, and even more in favour of getting to know all the regulars before moving on to the passage migrants and vagrants. April is a good time for resident birds, most of which are already singing and/or nesting. For a couple of weeks (depending, of course, on exactly where one lives) one can concentrate on these mostly familiar birds without being distracted by the winter visitors that have already departed, or the summer visitors that have yet to arrive. This is particularly important for beginners.

**Left** Knot occur in summer plumage for a few brief weeks in mid-summer. The birder who misses this treat must wait a full year to try again.

**Above** Snowy Owls breed in the far northern tundra zone. When the population of lemmings crashes, these birds come southwards in search of alternative food.

### Spring arrivals

The second half of April and first half of May see the main arrival of birds that have wintered, often in foreign climes, well to the south. Virtually every day sees more and more birds pouring in and there are new species appearing throughout this period. Many, like the Swallows, Warblers and Flycatchers, may breed nearby, but others may merely pass through on their way further north. This is an excellent time for identifying a wide range of birds, for most are in their summer finery, in plumages that show them at their best and which are seldom seen later in the year. Waders and shorebirds, in particular, are at their best, but so too are the Warblers that can cause so much of

a headache on their return in the autumn. As so many birds are singing lustily, this is also the best time to locate the scarcer or more secretive birds that breed about us.

In general, spring is not as good as autumn for producing rarities, but a phenomenon called "overshooting" regularly produces birds that breed further south. In fine, warm weather birds often fly straight over their normal breeding zones to appear in areas often hundreds and sometimes more than a thousand kilometres to the north. That is they "overshoot" their range. This is a phenomenon peculiar to spring and the major source of rarities at this season.

Soon things begin to quieten down as residents and summer visitors settle down to rear their young. A few particularly high-Arctic birds may still pass through during June on their way to the tundra wastes, which remain frozen until early July. But June is the month for watching breeding birds, enjoying bird song and seeking better views of the more elusive or hard-to-identify species.

By mid-July the countryside is full of young birds and there is a flush of Warblers that seem, already, to be on the move. By the end of the month there are even waders returning from further north as the vanguard of the masses that will pass through in August. For some peculiar reason August, at least in temperate north-western Europe, has gained a reputation as a poor month for birds. Yet nothing could be further from the truth. There are masses of birds in August. The Warblers, Flycatchers, Chats and Swallows are pouring through and the marshes are alive with a splendid variety of waders.

### Autumn migration

September brings the rarities and they include species that can be seen at no other time of the year. Many birds at this time may be only a short distance off-course and be of irregular occurrence rather than mind-bogglingly lost. This is also the time for the more regular birds to appear in

strangely inappropriate places and a grand opportunity to see all manner of birds in situations such as the local park or even your own back yard. By October the mass of birds has departed or passed through, but migration still continues and rarities turn up from all sorts of far flung lands. If a new bird for the country is to be added to the list it will probably occur in this month. Some will

have flown thousands of miles in the wrong direction - a process called "reverse migration".

### The birder's winter

Late October and November see massive movements, usually observed soon after dawn, of winter visitors pouring into the area. The wild geese and duck may be the most obvious, but there are often eruptions of northern birds like Crossbills, Snowy Owls and Rough-legged Buzzards. November also sees a passage of northern seabirds and a gale-blown coast may see "wrecks" of some of these species. By December, most of the regulars have arrived and it is usually the harshest weather of January and February that forces birds from further north to seek sanctuary to the south. Among these are high-Arctic birds that have been beaten southwards by extreme conditions. Most are seabirds and, whichever side of the Atlantic you inhabit, the prime rarity is Ross's Gull, a dainty, wedge-tailed Gull that lives along the edge of the pack ice.

March may be the month of departure for winter visitors, and it may produce a return movement of birds that have wintered to the south, but it is really the month when the earliest summer visitors arrive, bringing the first taste of spring and the new season to come.

**Left** To see Spotted Redshanks in their black finery is possible in June and July. To see them perched in trees requires a special journey to their northern breeding grounds.

**Below** Rough-legged Buzzards leave their northern breeding grounds on an irregular basis, depending on the population of small mammals.

# URBAN BIRDING: CITIES

Cities would not seem the most conducive environment in which to pursue birds, yet they remain the stamping ground for generation after generation of birders. Most start harmlessly enough watching the birds in the back yard, graduating to the local open space and then finding that the urban sprawl really has quite a lot to recommend it.

### The House Sparrow and Starling

The most adaptable birds are the most successful and, as we come toward the end of the 20th century, the most successful of all are those that can live alongside man. Nowhere is this more apparent than in our great cities. Some birds like the House Sparrow and Starling owe their entire success to man and the Sparrow, in particular, cannot be found where man has no permanent presence. Most birds, however, can find something approaching their natural habitat, be it a garden that resembles a woodland edge, or a park that is more like a partially cleared forest. Others find the similarity between our buildings and their natural cliffs quite satisfactory and some find the nooks and crannies in buildings so perfect that they have all but abandoned natural nesting sites completely. The important principle, and one that we have come across before, is that if a food source exists

some bird will have found a way of exploiting it.

In London, the age of horse-drawn transportation, with its consequent spillings of grain, created perfect conditions for House Sparrows and there is every reason to believe that these highly adaptable little birds prospered as never before. Then came the automobile, which spilt pollution rather than grain, and the Sparrows declined. However, just as they were able to adapt to city life in the first place, they soon found other sources of food and are now the dominant species

**Left** Kestrels are among the most attractive of the birds that have adapted to the urban environment. Basically mouse specialists, in many cities they have switched to House Sparrows as their staple prey.

**Below** Central Park, New York, offers a green oasis in a sea of concrete that draws migrant birds and their watchers throughout periods of passage.

at all urban bird feeding stations.

Just as the House Sparrow has found city life very much to its liking, so too have the European Kestrel and Tawny Owl. These typical cliff and woodland nesting birds are small mammal hunters, one catching its prey by day, the other by night. Though all cities have their share of small mammals, they are by no means abundant,

**Left** A male Black Redstart at its urban nest. These birds first colonized Britain during the Second World War, when the bombed sites of London offered a substitute for the burned over cliffs that they require.

especially in open areas where they are prone to air attack. Both Kestrel and Owl have adapted successfully to an urban lifestyle by changing their diet - from small mammals to House Sparrows. So the success of one species has led directly to the success of others.

### Habitats

A city is, however, much more than an aggregation of houses, shops, offices and factories. There are gardens, parks and ponds and there are railways and sometimes canals, running like arteries from countryside to city centre. There are markets and warehouses, factories and marshalling yards. There may be docks and wharfs and perhaps an airport. All cities need food, water and various methods of waste disposal and it is in meeting these needs that so many fine bird habitats are created. Birders have been quick to recognize the attractions of such urban habitats and reservoirs, rubbish tips and even sewage works have become concentration points for birds and birders alike.

In some ways, though totally geared to the urban environment, these facilities are almost small pieces of wild habitat surrounded by bricks and concrete. The city does, however, offer another habitat that is much less specific in its attractions. Offshore and isolated islands have

long been known as excellent places to watch for migrants and off-course vagrants. Fair Isle, between the Scottish Orkney and Shetland Islands, and Heligoland, off the coast of Germany, showed that such islands, surrounded by miles of inhospitable sea, have immense gathering power for small land birds. It took us much longer to discover that islands of green surrounded by seas of concrete could have the same effect. From Central Park in New York to Regents Park in London, and at a host of other green islands, birds seek an oasis in an otherwise hostile environment. Naturally, birders have followed. Doing the daily rounds during migration periods can be very rewarding, though in several seasons of working my local London park I did not see those rarest of Siberian waifs, the Yellow-browed and Pallas's Warblers - both seen by my successor! Yet on a trip to New York and a compulsory visit to the Museum of Modern Art, I was staggered to find a Hermit Thrush in the courtyard. Of course, these little birds are regular in urban open spaces, but the courtyard of this Museum has only half a dozen small trees growing in pots and is surrounded by concrete and glass cliffs that tower into the sky on all sides. In effect the bird must have made a virtually vertical descent of well over a hundred metres to reach its tiny patch of green.

# DERELICT SITES

**Left** House Martins construct their nests under the eaves and ledges of buildings, whether they are occupied or derelict. This bird has partly constructed its nest, but must wait for each layer of mud to dry before adding a further course.

**Below** Little Owls are typical birds of wasteland where they find the ill-kempt landscape a happy hunting ground for the large insects on which they mainly depend.

When asked what opinion was formed of a particular city, it is easy for a visitor to say "It will be lovely when it's finished"! Sadly cities are never finished and construction is followed by demolition in an endless series of redevelopments. There are always derelict sites awaiting development. Many are converted to car parks for an interim period, sometimes for several years, while the planners and developers debate their various schemes. But some are left derelict, even uncleared, for a generation or more because their original function has been made redundant. The old docklands with their cranes and wharfs are classic cases of changing technology making whole areas of cities redundant almost overnight. Cargo ships have been replaced by container ships, dockers by mechanical handling. The waters that remain, with their surrounding, overgrown open spaces, become a peaceful haven.

### Demolition sites

The dynamics of redevelopment, in all its various forms, offer fresh opportunities to birds and wildlife. Taken out of continuous human use, it is

surprising just how fast nature can reassert itself. A crack in a concrete slab offers a home to mosses, grasses and a few "rough-ground" flowers. Buddleia, beloved of butterflies, appears from nowhere and grows within a year to surprising proportions. Insects and other vertebrates quickly follow the first vegetation and, with them, come the birds to feed on plant and animal food alike. Mostly they will be the more abundant birds of the neighbourhood, birds that have already adapted to an urban life-style, but others will follow. Some species actually prefer demolition sites.

During the Second World War, London suffered enormous damage as a result of sustained enemy bombing, especially during the Blitz. Huge areas were totally destroyed and the interior walls of terrace houses were exposed with wallpaper and fireplaces clinging bizarrely to a still-standing neighbour. These bomb-sites were shored-up and fenced off to provide the perfect habitat for colonizing Black Redstarts from the Continent. The cliffs of buildings, with their blackened chimneys, and the overgrown scrub of back yards offered conditions that these attractive little birds found ideal. London became the species headquarters in Britain. Even today Black Redstarts still appear (and breed) on the redevelopment sites of the city, though they have, more recently, found that power stations and railway marshalling yards are a more permanent home.

### Unexpected birding

Most birders are always on the look-out for new birding sites, particularly if they are handily placed near their home or work. To the gentlemen of Wall Street and the City of London, such a site can offer opportunities for birding in an otherwise rather bleak landscape. Some years ago I discovered a sewage treatment works and area of allotments that had been closed prior to redevelopment. It was only a tiny affair, but it was a virtual jungle, broken by old pools, buildings and pieces of discarded machinery. The surrounding houses and factories had no effect on the birds and a variety of different species were found breeding there. Similarly, during migration periods, the birds poured in and Warblers and Flycatchers could be seen among the vegetation. Sometimes there were even waders on the tiny pools. Frankly, there were no birds that could not have been found quite easily outside the city, but there were several birds that were decidedly scarce for inner London. Sadly the area was soon built over and is now a carpet warehouse, or some such.

### Privacy

I suppose part of the attraction to birds is the privacy of an isolated urban derelict plot. Because someone, albeit a giant corporation, actually owns the site and because such sites are generally dangerous, they are usually well fenced to prevent trespass. Such lack of disturbance is rare in the city and those places that can offer peace and quiet tend to attract and hold their birds better than the open spaces that have free public access.

One of the best examples of such privacy have been the traditional docklands that were obsolete but undeveloped. Many such areas now provide fashionable homes for city executives, but during the intermediate years the docks were a haven for birds. Duck found the quiet pools a wonderful refuge and roost, opening up feeding grounds that were previously under-used. Other water birds prospered too, as did a whole host of smaller species which lived among the surrounding buildings and quaysides. Today the docks have been developed as up-market marinas, but there may be areas of old docks that are still worth a birder's thorough examination.

**Below** The urban environment frequently offers new and unusual feeding opportunities to birds. These Great and Blue Tits have learned that foil topped bottles delivered to British doorsteps can be opened to provide cream.

# RUBBISH TIPS

One of the by-products of urban life is rubbish and, in general, the more affluent the society the more we have to throw away. Medieval townspeople simply threw their rubbish into the streets, where it was devoured by scavenging dogs, cats, rats and birds. We can see the same process today in small towns in Central America, Africa and Asia. Here vultures and kites boldly circle the buildings waiting to squabble over any vaguely edible titbit. To the local inhabitants this is normality, to the visiting birder the sight of so many birds of prey at short range is a real treat. Our own societies have become progressively more health and tidiness minded; we put rubbish in dustbins or incinerators and pay the council to remove it from our sight. We pay the same organization to clear up streets and parks. And we expect our food to be offered in neat plastic packages, with little or no sign of its origins. In less squeamish societies, animals are still slaughtered publicly, or in the open at slaughter houses where

**Above** Gulls found on landfills and dumps do not feed continuously, nor do they feed every day. These birds near Chichester, England, are totally oblivious of the trucks and compactors while they feed, though it is the arrival of a truck that brings them from their nearby loafing ground.

offal is thrown to the birds. Not surprisingly many such places attract more than their fair share of birds of prey and some have earned an international reputation among birders.

## Land-fills

Our own rubbish is taken from us by lorry and dumped, usually at specially licensed land-fill sites. Not all sites are allowed to accept household waste because of various difficulties that the dumping of putrescible (decaying) waste creates. At such a site huge lorries arrive virtually throughout the day to dump rubbish. Much is wrapping, mostly plastic, but paper figures highly and there are also scraps of food. The economics of running a tip are such that the operator needs to get as much rubbish into a particular site as possible and huge compactors with roughly spiked wheels drive backwards and forwards to crush the material into the smallest possible space. There does not appear to be very much that is edible, but huge numbers of birds frequent the dumps day after day. In areas where they still exist Vultures may gather in large numbers along with other scavenging birds of prey. In northern Europe and many parts of the United States, Gulls are the dominant birds and they often occur in huge numbers. For most of the time they sit around among the rubbish sleeping and preening, but when a domestic waste lorry arrives they descend on the contents in their hundreds. The compactor moving back and forth is part of the scenery and is almost totally ignored. Some birds seem almost to be crushed as they eat and it is surprising what they do eat. It is best to be spared the details.

**Left** The Red Kite is a regular visitor to rubbish tips, particularly where these are associated with slaughter houses. They are common birds on the Continent, but in Britain are still confined to central Wales.

**Above** Magpies have earned a reputation for thieving and they find rubbish tips eminently suited to their kleptomaniac tendencies.

### Gulls and dumps

The provision of food at dumps has attracted huge numbers of Gulls to lead an inland existence away from the coast that most of them are adapted to exploit. But cities have also provided another essential to this inland move - large freshwater reservoirs where the birds can safely roost for the night. The idea of thousands of Gulls spending their days trampling through and eating our rubbish only to fly off at dusk to spend the night sitting (and other things) on our drinking water does not sound altogether healthy. But I am assured that modern purification systems are so good that there is positively no danger.

Gulls and the more traditional scavengers are not the only birds that seek a living on the rubbish that we throw away. Crows, Starlings, Sparrows and many other smaller birds also make use of the food that we provide. In hard weather in particular, when snow and ice make more natural foods unavailable, a whole host of different species will take advantage of the open ground offered by rubbish tips. As it is filled, topsoil is placed over the pit in a somewhat futile attempt to pretend that it was never there. Initially, such reclaimed areas may quickly produce a bumper crop of weed seeds that attracts flocks of small Finches. Later they may be converted to grassland or a housing estate replete with methane gas!

Gulls are a potential hazard to modern jet aircraft and, in approving a particular site as suitable for waste disposal, local authorities must bear in mind the situation of airports and airfields.

# SEWAGE PONDS

In the early days of sewage treatment, the contents of the sewers were pumped into large pools where the solid material would sink to the bottom and the liquids were allowed to run off over adjacent fields; thus the origin of the term "sewage farm". The well-watered and well-fertilized fields produced a rich grass crop that was grazed by bullocks, thus providing a by-product to sewage disposal. The pools that collected the solid material gradually filled up and from time to time, depending on pumping operations, became splendid, if smelly, freshwater marshes. Birds are curiously immune to any sense of aesthetics and watching migrant waders at sewage works soon became an integral part of the urban birder's year. With so few other areas of open mud to choose from, these settling pools attracted the best variety of waders in most inland localities.

## Sewage and bird-watchers

Modern filter systems soon replaced the open grass fields, but settling pools remained an integral part of the system for many years - to the great joy of bird-watchers. Today even these have largely gone as we adopt a more mechanical approach to waste disposal. Even so sewage works still attract large numbers of birds, though these are mostly species that are well established in the urban environment. Starlings, always with an eye to the main chance, have found circular sprinkler filters a fine foraging ground. Perching on the rotating arms, they drop to the clinker for a quick snack before the next arm sprays them with dirty water.

**Below** The Wood Sandpiper is only one of a large number of waders that use sewage settling pools as handy migration stopovers during their journeys across Britain.

mud intersected by pools of water. They can be marvellous places for birds, though, like the sewage works, much depends on the pumping strategy of the individual works. Sadly, beet factories are not situated adjacent to large cities - most are sited among areas of rich arable land - but they do offer a refuge for waders and their watchers in areas that are otherwise devoid of good marshland.

### Dredging

One other industrial process also creates artificial marshland and is richer by virtue of being sited near the coast. Most great cities have their origins in being ports and many are sited at the mouths of rivers. As ships have grown bigger the survival of such ports has depended on deep channels. Some, unable to cope with larger ships, have fallen by the wayside or created an alternative form of success. Others have had to resort to dredging. Rotterdam, the world's largest and most successful port, is a

**Above** Little Stints are among the more regular birds seen at sewage works though, like the other waders, they occur only during migration.

**Right** Pectoral Sandpipers are American shorebirds that frequently cross the Atlantic to appear on European marshes. They are just as likely to turn up at a sewage plant as at a marsh.

Insects find these systems an excellent breeding ground and many birds, like the Wagtails, find a good source of food and may nest among the machinery or in the buildings nearby. Small migrants too may stop-over to feed.

Here and there an old-fashioned sewage works may still survive, usually serving a small, relatively isolated community. This is the place to look for waders at the settling pools. But even the larger works still have similar pools, though they are generally small and artificially banked tanks. These are favourite haunts of species like the Common and Spotted Sandpipers that pick, rather than probe, for food.

There are, however, other waste disposal systems that still use settling pools and which function in much the same way as the old sewage pools. Sugar beet factories produce huge quantities of liquid waste that is converted to solids by settling pools and a pump-off system just like the old sewage works. These artificial lagoons are often suitable for waders, with areas of drying

case in point.

Dredging deep water channels at the mouths of rivers is not only a continuous and expensive process, it also produces thousands of tons of unwanted silt. The usual method of getting rid of this is to pump it into lagoons alongside the estuary, creating wonderful brackish marshes which are absolutely perfect for waders. Being adjacent to what are already excellent wader habitats, these lagoons act both as feeding grounds and as roosts for the birds.

# OASES IN CONCRETE

when the area is confined by the sea, or a concrete sea, one has a feeling that one has probably seen all the birds that are present. In this way a daily visit can show just how the park is being used by migrant birds. Some days may be rather thin, but then there will be a small rush followed by a tail off until the next arrival.

At one time there were several of us in London each watching his own park throughout the spring and autumn. Each kept a daily tally of species and numbers and it was my job to draw all of these together and see what correlations could be made. Numbers, even of the commoner Warblers, were

**Left** London seems to offer hardly a break in the cover of bricks and mortar. Yet here and there tiny squares and gardens are quite capable of providing a haven for birds.

**Below** A migrant male Blackcap finds an orange discarded in a city park a useful source of food as it seeks to build its reserves prior to continuing its journey.

An island in a sea of concrete is a pretty apt description of a bird's eye view of a city centre park. Migrating birds, finding themselves over a city which might measure as much as 30km (20 miles) across, are faced with a sea of inhospitable concrete broken here and there by islands of greenery. And just as they will seek out land rather than alight on the sea, so they are drawn to parks rather than making a landing on buildings or streets. In New York, Central Park has long been known as a splendid area for birders to spot migrating Warblers, Flycatchers, Vireos and Thrushes, particularly in spring.

## Daily tally

Working a confined area during migration periods is remarkably rewarding no matter where it is, but

generally small, but it was surprising how the occurrence of high figures in one park coincided with similar figures in the others. Even the different species coincided quite well, showing that birds were flying over the city during quite specific periods. The nearest proper bird observatory was at Dungeness on the Kent coast, and the warden kindly sent me the daily tally for comparison. To my surprise even this fitted the pattern, with peaks and troughs of the common migrants fitting nicely together. To my chagrin there were, of course, records of rarities scattered through the season at this prime coastal site, none of which had come my way in London. Many were birds that I could easily have gone to see had I not been so preoccupied with my own local patch. But, for a while, the daily changes in the number of relatively common birds provided far more satisfaction than the sight of the odd rarity or two. Now I am fortunate enough to live in the country and the daily round takes me no further than a brief tour of the garden, farm buildings and hedgerows. Without being in any way special, this small area of southern England produces all the common migrants in varying numbers day by day.

Some parks may be too big for a thorough daily exploration, but a good walk around will show which areas are best for migrants. Try the pond for a start, especially if it has natural banks and a bushy island. One of my earliest attempts to explore the "Fair Isle in London" concept saw me watching just such a bushy island in a small pond at the same time as the park keepers were making a routine visit for some reason best known to themselves. Landing at one end of the apparently

**Left** From the air New York seems to offer nothing to any migrant bird. Yet even in this apparently inhospitable environment the occasional bird, like this Hermit Thrush (**above**), may find a city tree, where it can rest and recover, even if the tree is planted in a pot.

bird-free island they acted as unintentional beaters producing a string of different Warblers at the other end as I watched. Finally they flushed out a gorgeous spring male Pied Flycatcher. I never missed the pond again.

Bushy areas, particularly where avenues of low trees come together in a "cross-roads" are often more productive than solitary trees. The best section of all in my park was a "natural" area of birches and hawthorn creating a clump no more than 100m by 50m. Yet morning after morning this tiny patch of cover produced most of the regular

summer visitors to southern England and others besides. Willow Warblers and Chiffchaffs, Whitethroats and Lesser Whitethroats, Redstarts and Spotted Flycatchers all put in their appearances. Once even a Wood Warbler, always a scarce migrant, rattled away beneath the canopy. Sadly, this was always an awkward area to work - the ladies' and gentlemens' toilets were sited right in the middle.

If there is one piece of advice that can be offered to the potential park birder it is be persistent; don't judge a park on a single day, at the wrong time of the year and, in particular, don't compare it with a coastal hot spot.

# FRESH WATER: UPPER REACHES

Fresh water provides many of the richest of bird habitats, wherever it is found. From the bleak uplands, where it falls as rain soaking into the largely infertile peaty soils, creating bogs and pools, to the embryonic streams, rivers and flood plains nearer the sea, water is the very stuff of life. Young streams often carve deeply into the hills, tumbling over waterfalls, creating rapids among the boulders and shifting huge amounts of material as they pass. Gradually, their helter-skelter pace is lost and the torrent becomes a

**Above** The Dipper is a specialist of tumbling streams where it finds its food by wading and swimming in the fast flowing water. The silvery sheen is created by air trapped among its feathers.

**Left** The Common Sandpiper spends its summers along the margins of fast flowing streams, where its continuous bobbing seems to merge with the bubbling water.

stream sheltered by the woods that line the still deeply cut banks. This is all fine bird country, a nesting ground for species to which fresh, unpolluted water is essential.

### The foraging Dipper

This is Dipper country. Dippers are the only birds that habitually "walk" underwater. They have strong legs and feet, ideally suited to grasping rocks, and wedge-shaped bodies that allow them to use the force of the current to submerge and surface at will. Much of their time is spent on mid-stream boulders, where their tell-tale droppings indicate their presence, but they wade and swim in and out of the water in their search for aquatic insects and their larvae. In fact, Dippers are so

orientated to a water-tumbling habitat that they are quite unknown where there are no swift-running streams.

A typical pair may have a territory no more than a couple or three metres wide, but extending along some 3km (2 miles) of river. When flying from one end to the other, they are more likely to follow the bends over the water than to take a short cut through the surrounding woods.

Another tumbling stream specialist is the Common Sandpiper of Europe and its North American counterpart, the Spotted Sandpiper. With virtually non-stop bouncing of the whole body, these small waders pick their food from the shallow water margins where sand has been dumped by the youthful river. In many ways they

behave like avian trout, picking the hatching insects from the surface film as they drift downstream. Unlike the trout, however, Sandpipers are only summer visitors to the streams; they spend their winters along the shores of tropical rivers, lakes and marshes.

The shallow, clear waters are also the home of Kingfishers. Strangely, both North America and Europe boast only one species of this widespread family each. The Eurasian Kingfisher (is River Kingfisher a better name?) is a small, brightly coloured bird that shows as a vivid blue streak as it flies. The American Belted Kingfisher is much larger, grey and white and, one must presume, concentrates on larger prey. Despite their common English name, not all of the world's Kingfishers actually catch fish or live beside water.

**Tail bobbers**

One further species is also invariably found along streams, though it also occurs at weirs and waterfalls. While all Wagtails are more or less waterside birds, the Grey Wagtail is virtually confined, as a breeding bird at least, to fast

**Above** Harlequin Ducks are white water specialists that inhabit large rivers where they cascade among boulders. Their ability to survive such torrents creates a special niche that they have totally to themselves among northern Duck.

running streams. Like the Sandpipers, these are birds that seem in constant motion, wagging their tails in non-stop action. As Dippers are named after their "bobbing", that is "dipping" action, it is clear that all three common streamside birds share this curious need for perpetual motion. As birds seldom do anything for nothing it is, perhaps, the continuous movement of the streams they inhabit that makes moving birds less prone to predators than static ones.

Watching for these birds of tumbling streams is a relatively simple process. One can, of course, walk the banks, though many streams are simply too broken to make such an approach anything but hard work. By far the best bet is to stop at every bridge across a likely stretch of stream, look for tell-tale whitewash and wait patiently, preserving one's energies for more formidable quarry.

# LOWLAND RIVERS

As the streams tumbling down from the hills join together and enter a more gentle landscape, their nature changes. They become broader and alternate between shallows and deeps. There is greater opportunity for emergent vegetation to find a foothold and there are often neglected backwaters that the river has abandoned. The water is richer in minerals and a wider variety of insects, fish and other aquatic life can find suitable places to live. Some rivers pass through lakes, canyons, torrents and other obstacles that create habitats similar to those of their youth, but the volume of water is too great ever to be called a stream.

For the first time swimming birds can use the river, with Mallard rearing their broods along the gentle stretches together with Moorhens and Coots. While the Duck often nest on the river banks hidden among dead leaves, the two Gallinules actually construct their nests among emergent vegetation. Here both old and new growth provides a stable base and plentiful cover. Even more secretive is the Little Grebe, which attaches its floating nest to an overhang or snag and covers its eggs with debris before leaving the nest. Time and time again a glimpse of one of these dainty swimmers is followed by its complete disappearance as it submerges never to be seen again. Little Grebes are masters of breathing, unseen among even the flimsiest vegetation.

### Kingfishers

Here, where the water is clear and the current swift, but not tumbling, Kingfishers are at their most numerous. The river is strong enough to cut into its banks, to provide breeding sites for the 'fishers, but not so dirty that the birds are unable to find their prey. Where the river reaches a natural barrier, where the waters tumble among rocks and over shingle, Mergansers may be found feeding on trout and salmon and making enemies of fishermen. Both Red-breasted Merganser and Goosander (Common Merganser) are perfectly adapted to catching fast-swimming fish beneath the surface of the water. Propelling themselves with large webbed feet, their highly streamlined shape speeds easily through the water.

In Europe it is confined to Iceland.

These are tough little birds that spend the summer among the roughest waters at the base of waterfalls and among the most awesome of rapids. They dive for food, but often swim furiously upstream simply to maintain their position in the rushing water. In fact, they are superb swimmers, using the currents and eddies to great advantage in their search for food. In winter, most birds move to the nearest coastline and, here too, they are found among boulders at the foot of cliffs where the waves threaten to beat them to death. In this way the Harlequins have a niche all to themselves, like the Torrent Ducks of South America.

All these birds, even those that live among the white water, need substantial rivers, not the higher but less fearsome streams of the hills. Inevitably there is some overlap, with species that occur in both younger and more mature rivers, but larger waters produce more food and the chain that starts with subaquatic vegetation and the insects that live on and among it, and that passes through crustaceans to fish, produces a much greater variety of life.

**Far left** The bright blue back is often the only mark seen as the Kingfisher speeds upstream. A series of hard winters have seriously reduced its population and it is now absent from many of the rivers and streams that it previously inhabited.

**Above** Goosanders are essentially river birds during the summer, building their nests in cavities nearby. Sadly, they feed on young trout and salmon and are widely regarded as enemies by fishermen.

**Above** Moorhens prefer the slower, more mature rivers, where a good growth of emergent vegetation acts as a hiding place for their bulky nests.

### Harlequin Duck

One of the most characteristic birds to inhabit the larger rivers is the Harlequin Duck, though sadly this bird is confined to the more remote areas of both Europe and North America. It winters along both Pacific and Atlantic coastlines, but only in the east does it wander far from its breeding grounds.

# PONDS AND LAKES

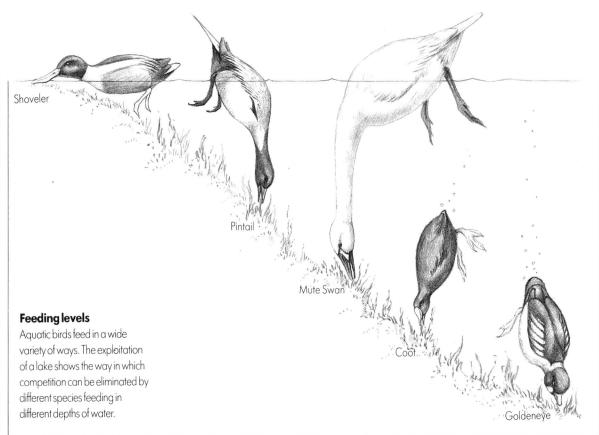

Shoveler

Pintail

Mute Swan

Coot

Goldeneye

**Feeding levels**
Aquatic birds feed in a wide variety of ways. The exploitation of a lake shows the way in which competition can be eliminated by different species feeding in different depths of water.

Fresh waters are among the best areas for watching birds, wherever they occur, simply because they are rich in life and offer a refuge away from terrestrial predators. Yet they vary enormously in the birds they hold and, therefore, in their attractiveness to watchers. In every part of the world there are examples of places where birds pick out one lake and ignore another that, to our eyes, looks equally inviting. A careful study may reveal that one lake is deeper than the other and thus offers feeding of a different type and quality; that one has more emergent vegetation that provides food and refuge for a wider and more abundant variety of prey; that one has a predatory or dominant fish that is lacking in the other; or that one is more disturbed. Even taking, or attempting to take, such factors into account, it is often difficult to decide why one water is used by birds while another seems to be avoided.

Ponds and lakes also vary in origin and size.

When does a pond become a lake? In the far north, an aerial view shows more lakes and pools than actual dry land. Of course, we expect snow and ice to melt each spring to produce marshes and rivers, but it is easy to forget that at these latitudes the ground beneath remains permanently frozen. This permafrost, as it is known, acts as an impermeable layer just like clay and the tundra pools remain right through the long days of the summer months.

**Arctic waters**
Though they are frozen solid for much of the year, in summer these Arctic waters are alive with insect life. Not for nothing is Lake Myvatn in Iceland, for example, known as the Lake of Flies. Such a wealth of life inevitably attracts predators and birds, by virtue of their mobility, are well adapted to take the advantage. Many of these lakes and pools are shallow and more akin to marshland, but some

may be quite deep and, like Myvatn, offer a summer home to thousands of birds.

Further south, where there is no permafrost, lakes may be fewer, but they then rest on an impermeable bed of rock or clay and are permanent, year-round waters. They may be home to divers (Loons), Grebes and Duck which are still, nevertheless, summer visitors. Many find their food by diving beneath the surface, while others search the surface or banks for their prey. Divers, as their name implies, are highly adapted to an underwater lifestyle. They have thick, insulating and waterproof plumage, a highly streamlined shape and powerful legs and feet set well back on their bodies to provide underwater propulsion. In fact these "paddles" are so well positioned for swimming that they are almost useless on land and the birds can only scrape themselves ashore on their breasts. Underwater they are magnificent and regularly remain submerged for a minute or more. This makes them highly efficient fish-hunters, but this ability is also used to escape a close approach by bird-watchers. A couple of lengths underwater is no problem and a diver will often put a hundred metres or more between itself and an intruder before surfacing.

## Grebes

Grebes are more varied in their requirements, for while some are decidedly northern in distribution, others are capable of exploiting a wide variety of different waters. Their main requirement is a plentiful supply of emergent vegetation and lots of food in the form of small fish. In winter, the need for lakeside vegetation is less crucial and these birds can be found on virtually any sizable stretch of water.

Like the divers, Grebes are expert fishermen and just occasionally they offer an opportunity to study their fishing techniques in a way that is all but impossible with the divers. A gin-clear lake in summer, inhabited by a pair of Grebes, especially a pair with newly hatched young, can be a delight. I have a vivid remembrance of one of these greensleeved waters in Hampshire, fed by one of the lovely chalk streams with which southern England is blessed. A Little Grebe was diving some 25m from the bank and emerging virtually in front of me. With polaroid glasses I could watch it dive and swim into the shallows at great speed, hugging the bottom of the pool as it came, as if below the

"radar" level of its prey. Suddenly there were flashes of silver everywhere as it rushed into a shoal of prey. Then it bounced to the surface with silvery fish in its bill. For almost half-an-hour I watched as the Grebe used the same tactics in the same place over and over again.

## Ducks

Some lakes are deep and others are shallow. In general the deeper the lake the less underwater vegetation and animate life it will support. Some lakes are so deep as to be virtually devoid of life except around their margins and they hold fewer birds as a result. Lakes that vary in depth may well hold both surface-feeding and diving Ducks. A large gathering of diving Duck indicates that a lake is rich in food and that it is neither too deep, nor too shallow. In Europe such gatherings mostly consist of Tufted Duck and Pochard, in America of Redhead, Canvasback and Lesser Scaup. Both Tufted Duck and Pochard, for example, prefer

**Above** Pochard gather in winter on large stretches of fresh water, where they dive to reach their almost totally vegetarian food.

medium-depth waters, but while Tufted take mainly animal food, Pochard are predominantly vegetarian.

Around the edges of such waters, or in the shallow and sheltered bays, there may be groups of surface-feeding Ducks such as Mallard, Shoveler and Pintail. But, just as the diving duck can feed happily side by side, because they take different food, so too are there distinctions in the food and feeding of these related birds. Shoveler, with their huge spatulate bills, sieve food from the shallowest of margins; Mallard often up-end to reach food below the surface; while Pintail up-end most of the time and have longer necks that enable them to feed on food that is out of reach of Mallard and all other surface-feeding Ducks.

Ducks do not, of course, have such waters all to themselves. Often they face competition from other birds such as Geese or Swans, which are even better endowed when it comes to neck length than the Pintail. In fact, the Swans fill the gap between the Duck that up-end and the Duck that dive, being able to reach a metre or more below the water's surface with a full up-ending technique.

Ponds and lakes are not, however, purely for the swimmers. Several other birds manage to make a good living from them without being able or preferring not to swim. Among the most obvious of these are the Terns, summer visitors that spend the harsh months of winter in milder climes. In general these tend to be coastal birds, but both Common and Black Terns breed inland on lakes. Common Terns dive for their food and can be regarded as competitors of the Grebes in their search for small fish. Hovering above the water, they focus in on their prey, before dropping head first into the water. Most prey is taken near the surface and the Common Tern seldom actually submerges completely. In late summer, when insects are hatching, these birds will also "hawk" for food, picking insects delicately from the surface as they struggle into the air. In using this technique they resemble the Black Tern, which is an insect-eater throughout the year. This graceful and masterful flier twists and turns as it dips delicately into the wind to pick item after item from the surface. Just occasionally, and probably under duress, Black Terns will dive for food, but their particular niche is the surface film of lakes and ponds.

**The Osprey**

One further specialist lakeland bird deserves more than a passing mention - the Osprey. This is the most aquatic of all the world's raptors, for while

**Left** Black-throated Divers breed near the water's edge of northern lakes. They are clumsy birds on land that can barely manage the few steps between nest and water, but they are expert swimmers and can disappear underwater for minutes at a time.

**Above** Slavonian Grebes frequent northern lakes in summer. The prominent golden head tufts in summer plumage are responsible for their North American name of Horned Grebe.

**Right** A pair of Great Crested Grebes virtually stand on the water, with head tufts raised in nuptial display. These birds of large lowland lakes have prospered under 20th-century protection.

various fish- and sea- eagles regularly take food from the water, they are all capable of becoming scavengers if the opportunity arises. The Osprey, however, is a master fisherman, as well as one of the most widespread of the world's birds. Its technique is to hover over a lake, locate and select prey and then to dive from a considerable height, crashing through the surface with feet and head almost together. Its long and sharp talons grasp its prey, backed by specially serrated toes that hold slippery prey quite firmly. Despite the power of its hold, fish actually die of suffocation as they are carried away in the air. Fishermen see the Osprey as a competitor, but Ospreys only exist where prey is plentiful and are an indication of the wealth of a particular water, rather than a threat to sport.

Many other birds find lakes attractive as feeding grounds, from the waders that pause on migration around their shores, to the Swallows and Martins that feed on the insects as they rise from the surface. In bad weather in particular, the insect life of our ponds and lakes may often play a crucial part in the battle for survival.

# RESERVOIRS

Reservoirs have been constructed since the beginning of civilization. At first they were needed as a store, to overcome seasonal drought and for use during times of siege to provide water for man and his animals. Only comparatively recently were reservoirs constructed to provide power and for other industrial purposes. Over the past 100 years, the number and, particularly, the size of reservoirs has changed dramatically. In hill and mountain regions, whole valleys have been dammed and flooded, creating vast lakes many miles long and often of considerable depth. These giant artificial waters provide hydroelectric power, as well as

**Below** A Trumpeter Swan adopts a threatening attitude toward an intruding scientist. Once virtually extinct, these natives of North America have been the subject of several reintroduction schemes.

**Right** Young Grey Phalaropes like this one may spend their first few weeks on some marshy bog, but are soon on their way to a winter swimming the southern oceans.

water, to fuel industries and cities, often at great distance. In some areas whole river systems have been converted to a series of man-made lakes. The Tennessee Valley scheme is still a monument to Roosevelt's "New Deal" of the 1930s.

Cities and industries consume the most enormous quantities of water and, in the second half of the 20th century, even the lowlands are not immune to reservoir construction. Rich agricultural land, often along the floors of large river valleys, has been flooded by giant waters, many times the size of a viable farm. Mostly these are artificially enclosed by earthworks lined on the inside by concrete to prevent wave erosion. Being so near large cities, these reservoirs have attracted urban birders and led to the "concrete-bowl" school of bird-watching.

## Upland vs lowland reservoirs

In general, deep upland reservoirs hold comparatively few birds, whereas lowland waters are mostly shallow and rich in life. Over the years

the latter have become refuges for wildfowl, major inland Gull roosts and important stop-overs for migrant wetland birds, from waders to terns and from Grebes to Wagtails. Some waters have become so important that they have been declared nature reserves, with significant populations of what are otherwise scarce birds. A series of reservoirs in southern Poland has complemented natural lakes to open up huge areas to birds and are now of international importance. Two lakes near Rheims in France have become the winter home of European Cranes and White-tailed Eagles; but most lowland reservoirs are best-known for their populations of Duck.

In many parts of England, for example, Duck may number several thousand on an individual lake; some may use the water as a feeding ground, others as a roost. In both cases, the birds are able to move into an area where they were previously

unknown in great numbers. Concrete bowls tend to hold mostly diving Duck, whereas natural banked lowland waters also harbour surface feeders along with Swans and Geese. The latter also tend to hold more waders, their natural banks offering better feeding opportunities, particularly in autumn when water levels are lower. From time to time reservoirs are pumped dry for maintenance and they may then resemble a marsh, with all of the bird opportunities that such a habitat offers.

During passage periods, Terns may pass through on their way to and from their breeding sites. They are usually more numerous and stay off-passage longer in autumn, and some reservoirs are noted for the number of Black Terns they hold at this time. Common Terns too may use them in this way and, in Europe, Little Gulls may gather in sizable flocks.

**Above** Black Terns spend the summer on shallow marshes, where they lay their eggs on a floating platform of vegetation. In full summer plumage they are unmistakable; in autumn and winter they are easily confused with other marsh Terns.

Being so near large cities, reservoirs are in great demand as water-sports centres. Fishing, sailing, water-skiing and sub-aqua have all boomed in popularity along with bird-watching. Sadly for the birds, these enthusiasts are prepared to pay to enjoy their sport, whereas birders have a noted reluctance to part with money. Many fine bird waters have been lost as a result. Happily, bird-watchers have the conservation lobby behind them and water sports enthusiasts have not had *carte blanche* with near-city waters. Nevertheless, water authorities are becoming progressively more commercial in their outlook and both birds and their watchers may, in the end, lose out.

# MARSHES AND FLOODS

In our increasingly populated and mechanized society, marshes and floods are regarded as unproductive wasteland, ripe for drainage and control. Even contemporary food surpluses have done little to stem the tide of "progress", though a more environmentally aware bureaucracy now at least pays lip service to the need to preserve natural habitats. Being shallow, marshes are prime candidates for conversion to agriculture, though there are some poignant examples of drainage schemes that have failed to produce the goods. Many remain wet and unusable, while others have become overgrown thickets of little use to anything. Yet marshes and floods are some of the richest habitats on earth.

Basically a marsh is an intermediate stage between a lake and a wood. Vegetation thrives, clogs up watercourses and is colonized by reeds, then by willows and alders and finally by birch and more substantial hardwoods. To create a marsh is relatively easy; to maintain it requires both control and hard work. One of the best examples of this can be seen along the Suffolk coast in England.

### Created marshes

Fearing an invasion during the Second World War, the British government decided to flood several low-lying areas of poor grazing to prevent a landing by enemy troops. By blocking drainage channels and sluices, the area between Walberswick and Sizewell was turned into two huge marshes separated by the crumbling cliffs of Dunwich. Although largely out of bounds, it is clear that many marshland birds responded with appropriate gratitude. Soon Avocets were breeding in Britain for the first time in years and, at the end of the war, there were Bitterns, Marsh Harriers and

**Left** Reeds like these only grow in shallow fresh or brackish waters. In many parts of Europe and North America reed beds have been drained for agriculture creating problems for many birds .

**Below** Black-crowned Night Herons are typical marshland birds that frequently feed in the poor light of dawn and dusk. They make regular twice a day flights between their feeding and roosting areas.

Bearded Tits all breeding in what had formerly been a quite unsuitable habitat. The Royal Society for the Protection of Birds (RSPB) quickly acquired the southern marsh as their Minsmere Reserve and have, over the intervening years converted this splendid area into one of Britain's top bird reserves. The northern marsh at Walberswick

remained in private hands and gradually became totally overgrown by reeds, then by increasing areas of willow. Minsmere had the birds and bird-watchers flocked to see them, virtually ignoring Walberswick altogether. Before this lovely marsh totally disappeared, the British government's conservation organization, the Nature Conservancy Council, acquired the area and active management has restored Walberswick to one of the finest reed marshes in the country.

**Transition to fresh water**
Near the sea, indeed just behind the sea wall, lies a series of shallow, brackish pools where migrant and breeding waders find a home. Here too there are Terns and Plovers, though a lack of privacy limits their breeding success. Inland, the lagoons become fresher and less disturbed, but rough grass is constantly invading and relatively few birds find conditions suitable for breeding. Still further away from the coast, the reeds become dominant and here there are birds galore. Pools have been opened out and created, giving many species a sanctuary away from prying eyes. Maintaining the marshland is an exacting job, especially when money is short .

**Above left** Spoonbills rear their young in tree-top nests, often alongside Herons and Egrets, where they are safe from predators. These birds are totally dependent on shallow marshes and are now found in only a few major colonies in Europe.

**Top** Great White Egrets not only need marshes in which to feed, they actually nest among the reeds, often over water.

**Above** Bearded Tits, like this male, are found only among extensive stands of reeds in freshwater marshes.

Man has always wished to command the waters and there have been many ingenious attempts to control the floods that regularly afflict many lowland areas. Floods are, in reality, no more than seasonal marshes that dry out in summer leaving only a few damp patches where waterbirds can feed. In winter, they are an invaluable home to Duck, Geese, Swans and waders which may sometimes gather in their thousands. The Ouse Washes in Cambridgeshire often hold thousands of Wigeon and wild Swans on their shallow waters, though by May they are dry and the birds have gone. There are, however, some birds that only breed among the damp patches of flooded grassland and the Black-tailed Godwit has made this area its headquarters since it recolonized

Britain during the course of the 1950s.

Quite recently, I explored the former Laguna de la Janda in Spain, a rich agricultural area in summer, but a splendid flood in winter. Here too there was a wonderful collection of birds, though the constant echo of gunshots was a reminder that birds need more than the right habitat to make any area their home. Yet even among the floods there were towering irrigation machines waiting to come into their own during the long hot days of summer.

Watching birds on freshwater marshes is one of the most exciting forms of birding. Marshes are rich in both the number and variety of birds they support and invariably hold some species that are either rare or decidedly local in distribution. Watching over a reed bed will produce Duck, Warblers, Bittern and the occasional bird of prey, but where there is open water with shallow muddy edges there may be literally thousands of Ducks, Waders and other species. Such watching needs a comfortable vantage point and one of the most dramatic changes during the past 30 years

has been the creation of a remarkable number of marshland bird reserves complete with hides.

### Scanning a marsh

For the beginner, entering a hide overlooking a rich bird marsh can be a thrilling moment. There are birds everywhere and the sheer spectacle is reward enough. Yet the thrill quickly wears off and the inexperienced show a surprising tendency to move on to another hide or another area in search of yet more birds. To the experienced birder the thrill is not the spectacle, but the opportunity, a chance to settle down and carefully, even meticulously, examine each and every bird. This may take an hour or more, for birds are continually on the move, appearing and disappearing, flying in and flying out. Some birds may be partially hidden and show little by which they can be identified; others may be too distant. Then, just as the task is being completed, a raptor may appear and send all the birds into the air. It is a dramatic sight that a beginner would adore, but which may be daunting to the experienced watcher who has got to start his search all over again. However, stirring the birds up in this way will bring some that were previously hidden or obscured out into the open

**Below** Eurasian Wigeon are among the most numerous of ducks found on freshwater marshes. They also regularly flight to dry land, where they feed on short sweet grasses.

and, perhaps, reveal a species that had formerly not been visible.

Scanning a marsh thoroughly is both an enjoyable and rewarding experience. It may produce a rarity, though usually it does not. The main attraction is the exercise itself, for trying to identify each and every bird present is a test of both ability and concentration. Ultimately, it is what all beginners should aim at - being able to put

a name to any bird seen anywhere.

From a birder's angle, the most attractive birds at any marsh are the waders. These birds are generally brown, similar in structure and often separated by the most subtle of differences. Some, like a Curlew, may be long-legged and long-billed, others may be squat and short-billed. The vast majority are passage migrants most numerous in autumn, when many are in juvenile plumage. In fact a thorough understanding of the seasonal plumages of these birds is often essential if every individual is to be identified. Once upon a time, field guides were full of warnings about identifying many of these birds and "inseparable" was a commonly used phrase. Today we may work on finer differences and warn beginners to take the greatest care, but we do have criteria for picking out the most obscure birds.

### Identifying waders

Perhaps the greatest challenge in wader identification is to separate the New World "peep" and the Old World "stints". This is a group of closely related small waders that can cause real headaches to the unwary. I have seen young birders cast an eye over a marsh and describe every bird present as a "Little Stint", while I was still busily seeking identification features on an autumn adult. As it turned out they were correct, but their verdict was far too fast to be reliable and they may well have missed the one bird that would have made their day - or their year, come to that. Speed in identification, particularly where waders are concerned, is not to be encouraged.

Given any choice at all, most birders would opt for a day at a first-class freshwater marsh in preference to any other habitat. It is perhaps the certainty of seeing birds that makes them so attractive, but there are birds that are never seen anywhere else. Some birders are quite happy spending the whole day watching a particular pool, noting the comings and goings as birds pause along their way. For the beginner the freshwater marsh may be a revelation.

**Left** Despite their extremely long legs, American Black-necked Stilts usually inhabit shallow marshes, where they build their nests on hummocks.

**Below** Damp, marshy grassland is required by the breeding Black-tailed Godwit, seen here in summer plummage.

# SALT WATER: CLIFF COLONIES

The sea has always had a magnetic effect on birders and many a long hour is spent peering out in search of birds that may only occasionally be seen along the shoreline. Such sea-watching regularly produces surprises, particularly during passage periods with a favourable onshore wind. Birds that were, only a short time ago, regarded as exceptional have been shown to be regular offshore, but for most of us the term seabirds conjures up pictures of cliffs packed with breeding birds, their wild cries echoing off the buttresses.

## Cliff colonies

A seabird cliff is one of the greatest of wildlife sights, to be compared with the migration of the herds of game across the Serengeti, or the massive tern colonies of some tropical island. Both North America and Europe are well endowed with such sights; from Alaska to Labrador, to Iceland, Britain and Norway, are some of the most splendid seabird cliffs in the world. At first one's eye is drawn to the milling mass of birds in the air, white Kittiwakes and grey Fulmars. Then one sees the lines of Guillemots (Common Murres) huddled shoulder to shoulder on the ledges. Razorbills are more scattered, while Puffins concentrate on the

**Left** The endearing Puffin, here seen with a neat billful of fish, is a cliff nesting bird that excavates its own burrow in soft soil on cliff tops and landslides.

**Above** Where they are separated by the sea from the mainland, Guillemots will nest on the flat tops of stacks. Kittiwakes construct their nests on tiny ledges.

cliff tops and among the grassy landslides, and Black Guillemots perch among the boulders at the foot of the cliffs. Where a huge scree runs down to the sea, there may be Shags, while some of the lower and broader ledges hold their close relatives the Cormorants. This is the average North Atlantic seabird colony with several thousand birds bringing a stretch of a kilometre or so of cliff alive.

More scattered are the colonies of Gannets, huge black and white seabirds that pack together usually on isolated stacks and uninhabited islands. The world's greatest gannetries are located in the Gulf of St Lawrence and around the rocky coasts of Scotland and Wales. The largest is on the St Kilda Islands off the west coast of Scotland where tens of

range of the Great Auk. Certainly it bred at St Kilda, at Papa Westray in Orkney, in the Faeroes, off Iceland on Eldey and the Westmann Islands and on the islands of the Gulf of St Lawrence and Newfoundland. The last known North American Great Auk was probably killed on Funk Island in 1794, while the last British bird was slaughtered on St Kilda in 1840. The last Great Auk of all was killed

**Left** Horizontal sedimentary rocks, eroded by wind and wave, create perfect ledges for Guillemots. With good feeding nearby, these birds may nest in thousands.

**Below** Razorbills prefer to nest among broken rocks where they can hide their egg in a cavity.

thousands white-wash the fearsome stacks.

In the far north Atlantic, other birds join the throng with Brunnich's Guillemot (or Thick-billed Murre) and Little Auk (Dovekie) often becoming the most numerous species. In the northern Pacific many of these cliff-breeders can be found again, though others are replaced by quite distinct species like the Horned and Tufted Puffins and by the auklets and the murrelets that are confined to that ocean.

### The Great Auk

One of the greatest of bird disasters was the extermination of the Northern Hemisphere's only Penguin. In fact, the Great Auk was not a Penguin even though it was a large flightless seabird and bore the scientific name of *Pinguinus impennis*. Actually, it gave its name to the penguins of the Southern Hemisphere, though it had disappeared before several species of these flightless birds had been discovered. No one knows the complete

on the island of Eldey, Iceland on 4th June 1844. Strangely, this last record concerned a breeding pair with a single egg: the adults were eaten, the egg was destroyed; the Great Auk was extinct.

It would be nice to be able to say that man has learned the lesson, but though the dangers are less direct, thousands of seabirds are slaughtered every year by poisoning, fishing nets and oil.

Meanwhile, many other seabirds are prospering and both Fulmar and Gannet have become much more numerous and expanded their ranges. From their stronghold on St Kilda, Fulmars have colonized almost the entire coastline of Britain as well as part of France and Norway. Their success has been attributed to food provided by fish waste from deep sea trawlers and that of the Gannet is usually ascribed to the same cause.

On the one hand man destroys, on the other he encourages, but living on a human dominated planet does place a responsibility on us to ensure the survival and prosperity of other life forms.

# DUNES AND ROCK BEACHES

Seabirds, whether they nest on cliffs or dunes, form colonies for protection and exist quite happily, often tightly packed together, because they find their food in a habitat where they cannot nest. The sea is available to all and, though the different species may feed in different ways and on particular foods, it cannot be divided up into territories. For the birder with a penchant for seabirds, a knowledge of these different niches is as important as a knowledge of where the great colonies can be found.

Many seabirds do not seek the safety of great cliffs, preferring instead to breed among dunes and beaches adjacent to the best feeding grounds. The various species of Tern are prime examples, but many Gulls also choose to nest in such areas. Watching a tightly-packed colony of Sandwich Terns is a splendid experience with all the bustle and noise, the comings and goings, the squabbles

**Below** A Little Tern arrives at its nest among the dunes. Increasing disturbance by | beachgoers has driven this delicate little bird from many of its favourite haunts.

and greetings that somehow epitomize summer birding. From time to time a sudden "dread" will lift all the birds into the air in a strange communal flight for no apparent reason. Sandwich Terns are particularly fickle birds that will nest in an apparently thriving colony for several years only to abandon it suddenly and move elsewhere.

### Common Terns

Common Terns never pack so tightly, but spread themselves out over the available breeding ground. Mostly they will be several metres apart, but still in touch with their neighbours and still leading an essentially colonial life. Just why one species packs so tightly together whereas a closely related species needs more elbow room is not fully understood, but there are clear advantages in nesting colonially. Terns may have well camouflaged eggs, but finding them is by no means difficult. The birds themselves are white, noisy and obvious and actually draw attention to their breeding sites. So instead of camouflage, Terns rely on aggression to deter predators. Deterrence is far more effective when would-be predators are confronted with several hundred furious Terns rather than the odd individual. As a general rule, birders should not disturb Terns at their colonies, but in more remote areas it is often difficult to know that one is entering a colony's domain until it is too late. Suddenly you are being dive bombed by angry and fearless birds with long sharp bills and Arctic Terns, in particular, can easily draw blood from an unprotected scalp. The answer is to hold a stick above one's head and beat a hasty retreat, but not everyone carries a stick so a tripod, woolly hat or anything else that offers protection can be forced into use.

Nesting on beaches has always had its associated risks; high tides can wash out a whole colony in a few brief minutes. Now, however, man has taken over the beaches and many birds find themselves invaded by scantily clad intruders just as their eggs are about to hatch. Little (Least) Terns have suffered a really serious decline in numbers almost entirely due to human intrusion at the wrong time.

At coastal bird reserves, action can be taken by fencing off particular areas and requesting the co-operation of summer trippers. But some wardens make a point of walking the beaches before the birds lay their eggs in an effort to persuade them to nest on safer ground - and it works.

### Gull colonies

Some of the largest dune-breeding colonies are of Gulls and many have been thoroughly studied over

**Left** Roseate Terns are among the rarest and most beautiful of all seabirds. Their white plumage, washed with peach on the breast in summer, picks them out from the other more abundant Terns.

**Below** Though they nest in a wide variety of different landscapes, the largest colonies of Herring Gulls occur among dunes. In Holland such a colony provided the ideal subject for the ornithologist Niko Tinbergen to study gull behaviour.

many years. In Holland the colonies of Herring Gulls have provided us with significant insights into bird behaviour and the often complex relationships between individual members of a colony. Niko Tinbergen's work on this species was instrumental in seeing much animal behaviour in terms of a simple stimulus-response relationship, an explanation that has had a serious impact on modern psychology. At colonies in the Mediterranean, these aggressive birds have prospered at the cost of the rare Audouin's Gull, which by the 1980s looked set to be a prime candidate for extinction. Yet at root this was a situation caused entirely by man. Herring Gulls are adaptable birds that are quick to exploit a new opportunity. With the growth of holiday resorts around the Mediterranean, and the correlated boom in catering and food wastage, the Herring Gull has increased dramatically. As its numbers grew, it took over more and more breeding sites and the less aggressive Audouin's was driven out and failed to breed. Having been responsible for the changed situation, it is reasonable that man should try to redress the balance, and at several colonies the number of Herring Gulls has been controlled and Audouin's Gulls have been able to

move back in peace. They are now on the increase once more.

This situation would never have arisen without the development of the modern jetliner, yet the manufacturers, airlines and tour operators do little if anything for conservation.

# BETWEEN THE TIDES

**Above** Purple Sandpipers are typical rocky shoreline waders that, even in the breeding season, prefer this habitat. With their dark plumage they are easily overlooked amid the tide wrack.

**Below right** Despite their name, Oystercatchers feed mainly on mussels that they open with their large orange bills. They are generally found along rocky shorelines, but also frequent estuaries and sandy shores.

Most of our coastlines are blessed with tides, the water rising and falling twice each day in a less than 24 hour cycle. The result is a special zone along the shore that is alternately covered and uncovered by the sea. As the tide sweeps in, all manner of marine creatures benefit from the planktonic life that it brings with it. Mussels, barnacles, oysters, anemones and hosts of other animals filter-feed on the riches and they, in turn, provide food for fish, crustaceans, sea urchins and other more mobile life forms in an intricate web of life. In fact, the land between the tides is one of the richest life zones on earth, many times more productive than even the richest farmland. Not surprisingly, a wide range of birds have taken advantage of the superabundance to find a special niche of their own in this no-man's land.

## Rocky shoreline

One of the more spectacular areas, and one that people find particularly attractive, is the rocky shoreline. Here, at low tide, are the rock pools and although the tide may move in and out only a few metres there are birds that find this particular rocky niche exactly to their liking. Turnstones find a rich source of food among the tide wrack, among

seaweed and in all the nooks and crannies. Despite their name and their propensity to turn over stones to see what tasty morsels are hidden beneath, they are highly adaptable birds that can feed in a variety of ways. In fact one erudite ornithological journal closed its correspondence columns to accounts of the Turnstone's food when bird-watchers reported bread, a pig's carcass and a human body. In Europe, there are several other species that exploit this rocky shore habitat including Curlew, Redshank and Dunlin. None, however, is so specialized as the Purple Sandpiper. These dark little waders are easily overlooked among the rocks and are seldom found away from the jumble of a tideline. Relying on their camouflage they are often very approachable. They search the rocks and seaweed for crustaceans, snails and periwinkles and form flocks a hundred strong in particularly favoured areas. Though essentially tundra breeders, they have been found recently well to the south, on both sides of the Atlantic.

Though Europe has but two major rocky shore specialists, North America has several more. In Alaska and along the west coast, as far south as California, there are two species of Turnstone. The common Turnstone there is called the Ruddy Turnstone, but there is also a Black Turnstone, which is similar in shape and structure, but which lacks the rich chestnut upperparts of the more widespread bird. Along this same west coast, the Purple Sandpiper is replaced by the Rock Sandpiper which is very similar in winter, but more closely resembles a Dunlin in summer. Finally, and once again confined to the west coast, there is the Surfbird, a chunky wader that is placed in a genus all its own. It mixes freely with the Turnstones, but breeds only in south-central Alaska.

### Sanderlings and Oystercatchers

Two other species also deserve mention, though neither is totally bound to rocky shore. The Sanderling is so specialized to feed between the tides that, in small flocks, it busily follows each wave in and out, feeding on the tiny animals that are left behind every few seconds. This feeding behaviour is so well known that beginners often have difficulty in identifying Sanderlings when they are found away from the beaches feeding in a different style. In fact, when they are in summer plumage, I have heard all sorts of suggestions as to their identity.

Like Sanderling, Oystercatchers are often found feeding among the rocks. Their massive orange bills are used to open mussels, which they attack in two quite different ways. Some individuals are smash-and-grab merchants that simply bash their way into the hard shells and have badly worn bill tips as a result. Others are more clinical in their approach, prizing the shell open and delicately severing the muscle (no pun intended) that attaches the mussel to its shell. Once again America has an extra species that is lacking in Europe. The Black Oystercatcher is resident along the Pacific coast, while the American equivalent of the Old World Oystercatcher is confined to the Atlantic.

# ESTUARIES

**Above** Avocets have a distinctive method of feeding. The uptilted bill is swept from side to side over the surface to disturb and catch its food.

Of all the intertidal areas none are so attractive to birds and bird-watchers as estuaries. Here the tide-line may move hundreds, or even thousands of metres between its highest and lowest points. The wealth of life is unbelievably rich, with a wide variety of crustaceans, molluscs, worms and so on being found in huge numbers. Birds are the major predators and some of the best estuaries may hold up to a quarter-of-a-million waders throughout the winter. Yet, despite such wealth, visitors wishing to see these birds must plan their trips with the greatest of care. Altogether too many beginners have, in their haste and enthusiasm, visited a renowned estuary at the wrong time. At high tide an estuary is covered with water, looks just like another arm of the sea and can be totally birdless. At low tide mud may extend almost to the horizon with a few unidentifiable specks at vast distance that may be birds.

### The right time

The right time to visit any estuary is about an hour to an hour-and-a-half before high tide. Then, as the tide comes in, birds are gradually pushed off the mud-banks. They feed along the interface where water meets mud and, slowly but surely, their food is covered by the incoming sea. As the tide covers the last feeding ground, usually right at the edge of the estuary, the birds fly off in flocks, gathering other individuals and flocks until there may be a mass of thousands in the air. Such flocks may wheel and tower in the air, turning this way and that, exposing first their dark upperparts, then their white bellies. This is dramatic birding and delights even the most hardened birder on a sunny winter's day.

### Roosts

Then, quite suddenly, a thousand or more birds will disappear; the local experts will know where. Waders form high-tide roosts when the sea has covered their feeding grounds. Such roosts must be safe from predators and from disturbance and are used year after year. Most estuaries have several roosts that may all be used at once, or at different times. Here the birds often pack tight together, snoozing or preening until the tide turns and they can feed once more. The safest roosts are often on quite small islands and every piece of dry land may be occupied by birds. Late-comers often wheel overhead searching for the tiniest of spaces in which to land. Eventually, they may just land on birds already present, with presumed resentment.

Watching and photographing birds at a high-tide roost is a superb experience. However, the birds need the peace, quiet and rest that roosting provides and it may be dangerous to disturb them. Fortunately several conservation organizations have established reserves on estuaries and in several places it is possible to watch over a roost from a hide without disturbing the birds.

**Above** Waders, such as these Knot, are driven from their estuarine feeding grounds by an incoming tide and fly to a regular high tide roost where they often pack tightly together.

**Right** Red-breasted Mergansers come in with the tide to feed on the fish that are themselves most active at this time.

### Daily cycle of waders
Waders on an estuary do not feed during the day and sleep at night like other birds. Their daily cycle is fitted to the tides. They feed when they can and sleep when they can't, no matter whether it's day or night. In fact, a visit to an estuary during a clear, moonlit night is an evocative if unromantic experience.

When the tide turns the birds will move away in large flocks, sometimes performing synchronized evolutions in the air. But they are usually keen to feed, and the post-roost performance is seldom as dramatic as that of pre-roost gatherings. Perhaps the most dramatic performances of all occur when a predator attacks a roost, particularly if it happens to be a Peregrine. These powerful raptors strike fear into almost anything that flies and flock reaction to a Peregrine may be spectacular. One cannot, however, rely on seeing a Peregrine attack, though these Falcons are frequently present at estuaries in winter.

### Other estuary birds
Waders are not the only birds that find a winter home among the mud and sandbanks of estuaries; Herons, Ducks, Geese and Grebes are also often abundant. Some feed among the mudbanks, others may feed on the incoming sea, others still on the surrounding land using the estuary as a handy roost. Brent Geese, or Brant as they are known in America, are the most typically estuarine of the Geese. Traditionally they feed on the eel grass that grows along the tidal edge, but the decline of this seaweed plus a general increase in numbers due to protection, has changed their habits. Today many Brent feed on agricultural land adjacent to estuaries and use the sea as a safe roost. Other Geese too feed in this way and roost in vast numbers on the tidal flats. Often the Geese's behaviour is the exact reverse of the waders' - feeding while the water is high and flying out to roost at low tide. Others maintain a more normal day and night routine.

## Ducks at estuaries

Many surface-feeding ducks also use estuaries as a roost and/or feeding ground. Mallard, the most adaptable, use them in every way and may be quite numerous where conditions are to their liking. Shoveler often pack at the tidal edge, sifting small particles of food alongside the pecking and probing waders. Pintail gather a little further out, up-ending in the shallow water, while Wigeon prefer to fly to the saltings and nearby grasslands to graze in tightly packed flocks.

It is, however, on an incoming tide that the largest numbers of Ducks are present on an estuary. Seaduck spend much of their time offshore in tight packs, or rafts, sometimes diving for food, but mostly dozing or resting. As the tide rises and all the creatures of the estuary become more active, the seaduck move in to feed in earnest. Truly monumental flocks of Scaup may come in with the tide along with packs of Scoter and Eider. There may also be Goldeneye and Long-tailed Duck, and even Mergansers and Grebes.

Mussel beds are a major attraction and at suitably rich feeding sites the Duck may gather in both number and variety. Factories, distilleries and

**Right** Shelduck are typical estuary feeders, using their large bills to sift through liquid mud in their search for the molluscs and crustaceans that are often so abundant there.

**Below** Brent are the most estuarine of all the Geese. They graze on beds of the seaweed zostera, but are also quite at home on nearby grasslands.

birds of prey. Peregrines were, at one time, called Duck Hawks in America and still are by many country people. It is, however, the often wild surroundings, the infertile and occasionally inundated land, that attracts the Harriers, Short-eared Owls and various Hawks and Buzzards. With these as highlights, birders find the estuaries an almost irresistible magnet.

Though this land between the tides is at its best in winter, it does have a distinct appeal at other times. In summer a few waders, Gulls and Terns may breed, but during passage periods a wide range of species may take advantage of the super-

**Above** Shorebirds frequently form mixed flocks on estuaries, especially when flighting between their feeding and roosting grounds. The long-billed birds are Godwits, but there are also shorter-billed Grey Plovers.

**Right** Turnstones are shoreline birds that feed on estuaries, as well as rocky shores, throughout the year. This bird is in summer plumage at Churchill in Canada.

breweries sited near estuaries all dispose of waste via outfalls that provide a rich living for underwater life. This in turn attracts the birds and any major outfall should be investigated. Twenty years ago, an outfall on the Firth of Forth near Edinburgh, Scotland, attracted up to 10,000 Scaup throughout the winter. Closing down the outfall has reduced this number to a mere handful.

### Predators
The number and variety of birds that use estuaries inevitably attracts predators and these include

abundance of food to stop-over and feed up for the long flights to come. In spring it may be Sanderlings and Ringed Plovers in their thousands, while in autumn there may be concentrations of thousands of Terns. Some estuaries are actually noted for the number of these birds they attract in autumn, and the Terns frequently attract numbers of attendant Skuas (Jaegers). These, usually offshore pirates, move in to rob the Terns giving watchers a unique opportunity to see their spectacular flying skills at close range.

# THE OPEN OCEAN

All the world's birds, with only a single exception, come to land to breed. The exception? This is the Emperor Penguin of the Antarctic, which breeds on the frozen sea itself. All other birds come to land to breed and so are within range of birders' binoculars. It is thus relatively simple to see any of the world's seabirds - you just visit their breeding grounds at the right time of the day and year. However, there are birds that occur off the coasts of both Europe and America that breed only on the most remote and inaccessible islands, out of reach of the vast majority of would-be watchers. Additionally, there are migrations of birds that

**Left** Manx Shearwaters come to land only to breed, and spend the rest of their year roaming the oceans, often well out of sight of land.

**Above** Long-tailed duck are purely sea duck in winter, occurring in large rafts usually within sight of land, but coming closer inshore to feed on a rising tide.

breed in more accessible areas, but which are seldom seen along the shoreline. Seabirds at sea are in their element and quite different to the often ungainly creatures they become on land. There are thus good reasons for watching seabirds off our coastlines.

### Sea-watching

In fact, sea-watching has enjoyed something of a vogue over the past 30 years and has added greatly to our knowledge of the lives of these often mysterious birds. Many, such as the Cormorants, Gulls and Terns are inshore feeders, seldom venturing far from land. Others, such as the Auks, go only as far as the Continental shelf, where shallow water enables them to feed. Some, however, are truly pelagic, spending most of their lives roaming the oceans. Among the latter, the various Petrels, Storm-petrels, Shearwaters and Albatrosses are the best examples. But Gulls, like

the Kittiwake and Sabine's Gull, the Gannets and Boobies and the Skuas are all ocean dwellers.

Because the oceans are featureless it does not follow that oceanic birds roam willy-nilly over their surface. The oceans are a maze of currents, of areas of warm and cold waters, of upwellings and of underwater features. Oceanic birds, like their terrestrial counterparts, have their favoured areas, follow seasonal migration routes and live a well ordered and largely predetermined life. Not surprisingly seabirds are most abundant where deep-sea fishermen have discovered the best fishing grounds, but the birds knew of them long before man.

### Headland sea-watch

Virtually any headland makes a good place for a sea-watch, but some are clearly better than others. Some, perhaps because the angle of the coastline suddenly changes direction, are good throughout any migration season. Others may need particular weather conditions to "blow" birds within sight. Among many coastal-based birders an hour's sea-watch may be no more than an ingredient in an otherwise dull and birdless day. Real enthusiasts head for the best sea-watch spots to be ready at first light when, for some reason, the best movements can be seen. The technique is to find a sheltered spot away from the worst of the wind, settle down comfortably with telescope and tripod at the ready, and scan the sea with binoculars. Often birds may be distant, but with the wind in the right quarter they may pass close inshore.

One of the world's top sea-watchers ranks St Ives Island in Cornwall, England as an outstanding spot. In autumn, south-westerly gales blow the birds from the Irish Sea deep into the mouth of the Severn Estuary. They take shelter along the lee shore and then beat their way out to sea around the protruding headland. It is amazing what has been seen from this single little spot.

However, taking a leaf from the book of American birders, there are now parties of British birders chartering boats to venture offshore in search of birds that are otherwise seen only when storm driven. Such trips regularly produce Shearwaters that have migrated from the Southern Hemisphere, birds from Biscay to the south and, if one is really in luck, Wilson's Storm-petrel. This dainty, long-legged black and white bird is abundant off the coasts of Antarctica, but then makes a huge loop migration that takes it along the eastern seaboard of the United States and across the Atlantic to the coast of Portugal and southern Spain. A few venture northwards to the Channel approaches, and the sea area between England, Ireland and France has become known affectionately as "Wilson's Triangle".

**Above** Eiders gather into considerable flocks at favoured feeding grounds. This tightly packed group has been disturbed while nesting.

**Right** Wilson's Petrels breed only in the southern hemisphere, but then make huge loop migrations into the North Atlantic.

# CULTIVATION: FARMS

Throughout Europe and North America, the forests have been cleared, grasslands ploughed, wetlands drained, heathlands planted and the whole natural landscape changed beyond recognition. Places that remain "natural" in appearance lie on poor, unreclaimable soils, or are areas that are too difficult to work profitably. Even here government aid has pushed back the frontiers of production with subsidies and other financial incentives to make the nation state as self-sufficient as possible. In terms of food production, such a policy is easily understood against an historical background of war, but the result has been gross overproduction and a drastic reduction even in the relatively few "wild" landscapes that remain. Throughout the lowlands the landscape now consists almost entirely of farms and farmland.

From a bird's angle, farmland can be divided into several distinct types: grassland; arable; orchards; hedgerows; and the few nooks and crannies that farmers find difficult to exploit. Nevertheless, huge numbers of birds live on farms, taking advantage of the special conditions created, or ekeing out a precarious existence along the margins of a farming economy. In North America farming is a comparatively recent phenomenon, at least over the larger part of the continent. The richness of the prairies could only be properly exploited after the building of the transcontinental railways in the 1860s and full development had to await mechanization by the tractor in the 1920s and 1930s. In Europe, the landscape has been changed over centuries.

**Left** The Lapwing is among the most abundant of grassland birds in Europe. Despite changing agricultural practices it manages to breed successfully in a variety of situations.

**Top** House Sparrows have prospered around farms where a shortage of nest sites may force many to build among bushes and trees.

**Above** Corn Buntings are locally abundant along grassland and arable hedgerows, although they are mysteriously absent in many areas.

## History of British farmland

In Britain, the feudal open-field system created an arable landscape broken not by hedges, but by furrows dividing the strip of one man's land from his neighbour's. Such open areas were broken by woods and marshes, by heaths and by the villages themselves. The first major change came when fields were enclosed for sheep in the great wool boom of the 16th century. This was, however, as nothing compared with the veritable agricultural revolution of the 18th century, which created the patchwork pattern of fields enclosed by hedgerows that we now regard as a typically English landscape. Imagine the effects of these changes on some abundant and widespread birds of this region. When woodlands covered large areas of England there would, doubtless, have been more Woodpeckers, Woodcock, Chaffinches, Nuthatches, Treecreepers, Jays and Sparrowhawks. Conversely there would have been fewer Lapwings, Mistle Thrushes, Blackbirds, Whitethroats and other birds of open land. With the enclosures came more open land with hedgerows to the benefit of the latter group and species such as Rooks and Yellowhammers.

## Recent changes

In recent years there has been a further change with the conversion of grassland to arable and the large field approach required by modern farm machinery. This has reduced the amount of grassland, with a consequent reduction in the number of birds such as Lapwings, while the reduction of hedgerows has had an effect on a variety of small birds that find this "woodland edge" habitat perfect for their requirements. Hand in hand with this change to arable farming has come the development of quick maturing cereals, the widespread use of pesticides and other "hi-tech" farming systems. As a result, it is increasingly difficult for many birds to utilize large areas of the countryside – a fact that is as true in North America as it is in Europe.

Ground-nesting birds have found mechanized farming and the use of short growing-period strains of crops virtually impossible to cope with. The once widespread Corn Crake has all but disappeared from the countryside where once its calls were one of the most characteristic sounds of summer. The Quail has followed a similar path of decline and the Stone-curlew will surely soon cease to breed on farmland altogether.

Birds that use arable land only as a feeding ground may well have increased, though modern sowing methods are less wasteful of seed and pesticides do eliminate pests, which are bird food. Rooks, for example, take both seed and pests and are generally regarded as more beneficial than harmful. They should have increased, but there is no evidence that they have done so. In fact, modern sowing techniques have brought a fresh species into conflict with farmers. The ground-nesting Sky Lark frequently feeds on the growing shoots of arable crops in spring. This mattered little when seed was over-planted and the growing plants were thinned in spring. Modern planting methods, using fewer seeds, makes the depredations of Sky Larks a serious problem. So even a minor change in technique can create a new situation that affects birds.

**Left** Barn Owls are nocturnal predators around many farms, though they do require breeding sites that are safe from disturbance. For preference they also need overgrown or neglected grasslands over which to hunt.

# GRASSLANDS

Traditionally, grassland is grazed by domestic stock and the major factor affecting grassland birds is the extent of cattle grazing, as against the short-cropped grass produced by sheep. The difference largely affects birds that are feeding, for even the disturbance of grazing animals prevents many birds from nesting on the ground. There are, however, differences between species. Sheep pastures are used by species such as Partridge, Stone-curlew and Wheatear, particularly when they are situated on well-drained, dry soils. Damper pastures, used mostly by cattle, are favoured by Redshank, Yellow Wagtail and Lapwing. So a change can have a marked effect.

### From hay to silage

Perhaps the most dramatic change to affect grassland birds in recent years has been the switch from hay to silage as winter feed for cattle. A traditional hay meadow was an area rich in wildlife and full of beauty, a haven for wild flowers, for nesting birds and for butterflies and other insects. Hay fields are home to birds such as Corn

**Above** Black-headed Gulls spend much of the winter feeding on farmland and are quick to exploit the opportunities provided by ploughing. Large open arable fields as well as grasslands are utilized by these highly successful Gulls.

Crake and Quail that have time to rear their young in safety over the long growing season.

Silage production differs in a number of ways. In the early part of the growing season the grass fields are heavily fertilized with natural and chemical fertilizers. Such disturbance often comes just as many ground-nesting birds are settling down to breed. Soon the fields are green with vigorous young grass, but before the grass can flower, the fields are mown and the grass picked up for clamping. A second grass crop is usually taken later in the season and the whole growing routine is far too short for ground-nesting birds to rear a brood successfully.

### Grassland opportunities

Grasslands vary enormously in the opportunities they offer to birds. Nesting birds require their

**Left** The Corn Crake has been unable to cope with agricultural change in most parts of its former range. Its familiar call is now confined to northern and western areas of Britain where modern machinery is less suited to the land.

**Below** Rooks are, in many areas, totally dependent on agricultural land, where they eat huge numbers of pests as well as some seed. On balance, they probably do more good than harm to agricultural interests.

grasslands to be largely undisturbed, even by domestic stock. In several places, conservationists have, with the landowner's cooperation, erected protective barriers around the nests of particular species. Such action can, however, have little effect on the overall populations of birds, save in a particular locality. The sympathy and understanding of farmers on a much wider scale is required if many of the birds that breed on grassland are to prosper.

When it comes to winter, grasslands and the birds they support are far less liable to disturbance and many birds depend on this habitat for the lean season. Some areas boast quite huge populations of Lapwings and Golden Plover. These species are just as likely to frequent dry upland grass as they are wet lowlands. Wild Geese also winter on grasslands grazing the fresh leys in preference to long established meadows. The Barnacle Goose is particularly fond of such grassland and has moved to leys, in preference to its original habitat of sweet dune grassland, wherever they are available. For these birds, grassland needs to be situated near a favoured roost, usually near the sea. Duck, such as Wigeon, are also largely grassland feeders and their numbers can be quite staggering.

Rooks, Jackdaws, Crows, Wood Pigeons, plus the Winter Thrushes are all regular grassland feeders, while the number of Gulls that spend their winter feeding on grassland probably exceeds those that feed on rubbish tips.

# ORCHARDS

From a bird's angle an orchard is no more than a well-ordered forest or a particularly large hedge. It differs, of course, in that there is usually no understorey and that the trees are all of one species. An overgrown orchard does, of course, become a thicket and offers a range of quite different opportunities to birds. Climate and underlying soil determine which areas are used as orchards, and it follows that orchards tend to be concentrated in particular areas. A change in economics or fashion can change radically the landscape of huge areas of land in a matter of a few seasons. The significant factor about orchards is that, while they can be destroyed in a few days, they actually take many years to establish and become productive.

Orchards inevitably consist of trees of a single age and though farmers pursue a policy of tree replacement, they never achieve a cross-section of ages. Thus in one apple orchard, all the trees will be of a particular variety of apple, all of the same age and more or less the same proportions. Nearby may be an old orchard, with a sprinkling of younger trees, but with the threat of clearance imminent. The older trees offer much greater opportunities for birds than the younger ones. The heavier the trunk, and the more gnarled and holed

**Below left** Hawfinches are often found in orchards and groves, but are always decidedly secretive and difficult to locate. Some birders may go years without seeing one.

**Above** Orchards, especially mature ones with old and gnarled trees full of holes, are a favourite haunt of Wrynecks. In England this bird is now no more than a scarce passage migrant, while in Scotland there are signs of a new colonization.

the branches, the greater are the opportunities the tree provides for both feeding and nesting. Most orchards are pruned vigorously each year to maximize fruiting and to improve the ease of picking. Trees with holes are often "filled" or replaced, but some are allowed to remain and offer splendid nest holes for birds.

### Mediterranean olive groves

Some of the most interesting orchards in Europe are the olive groves of the Mediterranean, populated by some of the oldest cultivated trees in the world. Generations of pruning may have limited their size, but they are frequently full of holes and can provide marvellous birding opportunities.

Olive groves may have an understorey of some crop, often cereals, but it is generally of poor quality. More usual is a natural crop of weeds and grasses creating opportunities for insects and birds. Such groves may hold Titmice, Finches and Thrushes along with Hoopoes, Golden Orioles, Flycatchers and Shrikes. In parts of southern and and western Iberia, there may be groves of cork oak nearby and, where olives and cork meet, there is often a fine collection of birds. Virtually all the Black-shouldered Kites of Europe breed in this habitat and there are often Bee-eaters and Rollers as well. Little Owls are the typical small predator, though rocky outcrops will offer a home to migrant Scops Owls.

## Plight of the Bullfinch

Orchards also attract some birds that prefer to feed on the trees themselves, rather than nesting in them or feeding on the insects they support. In some areas this may bring fruit farmers and birds into conflict. In Europe, the colourful Bullfinch is regarded as a prime enemy of fruit farmers because of its penchant for consuming the fruit buds just as they are about to burst into blossom.

As a result there is, in Britain at least, a special clause in the bird protection legislation that allows fruit farmers to destroy Bullfinches when they cause damage. Clearly the birds are only responding to an artificial superabundance of a favoured seasonal food. Research has shown that Bullfinches rely on the seeds of ash trees to survive the winter and it is only when the ash crop fails that they become a serious menace to fruit farmers. It is thus obvious that if the ash crop can be eked out beyond the flowering season, then less damage will occur. The recommendation is not to

kill Bullfinches when they are doing the damage in spring, but to cull them the previous autumn so that there are fewer birds to eat the ash crop during the winter.

Even this, however, may not be necessary for Bullfinches are loath to fly across even narrow open spaces, preferring instead to progress along a hedge or from tree to tree. So orchard owners intent on cutting down damage to fruit trees would be well advised to remove a single line of trees around the outskirts of their orchards to create a space that the birds will seldom cross.

Orchards, particularly old and mature ones, are excellent areas for birds and should be thoroughly explored wherever they are found. If there is any choice, the more neglected they are the better.

**Left** Cirl Buntings, like this male seen at its nest, are typical birds of Continental orchards but have declined rapidly in Britain. They are now regular only in Devon.

**Below** Spotted Flycatchers find the open spaces and park-like qualities of orchards perfect for their needs. These summer visitors to Europe take readily to open nest boxes.

# HEDGEROWS

Hedgerows appeared in Britain with the enclosure acts of the 16th and 18th centuries, but they were well established in southern Europe among peasant farmers long before. Many of these Mediterranean "hedgerows" are, in fact, no more than areas at the margins of cultivation where rocks could be piled to least interfere with farming activities. Some became quite definite dry stone walls, but most were (and still are) a jumble of rocks where vegetation can grab a hold. The more formal hedgerows further north were designed to prevent domestic stock from wandering and were carefully laid and maintained to provide a dense, thorny barrier. Often standards, mature oaks and elms, were allowed to develop as wind-breaks. In fact, the age of an individual hedgerow can be calculated by the number of distinct species of shrub it contains – the older the hedge the richer the wildlife it supports.

## Hedgerows as a refuge

Where large areas of land are devoted to crops and grass, hedgerows are an important refuge. They offer nesting and feeding grounds, as well a lack of disturbance to birds that see them as an extension of the woodland. Finches, Buntings, Warblers, Magpies and Tits all use hedgerows as a refuge; a place to feed, roost and nest.

The demand for national self-sufficiency in food has been responsible for the removal of hundreds of miles of hedgerows to provide a few more acres of cultivable land and, in particular, to allow the economical use of large machinery. Over a period of 30 or 40 years much of the traditional landscape has disappeared and, along with it, many of the birds of farmland. That destroying hedgerows and creating huge fields has been successful financially is beyond doubt, but the social cost has been high and there have been serious side-effects. In intensively farmed arable areas, fields have become so large that one farm abuts another in a huge prairie-like landscape. Soil erosion by the wind has become a significant feature of farming and wind-breaks have, of necessity, been planted to slow the process. The overall result has been to

**Left** In many parts of Europe Chaffinches are the most abundant of hedgerow birds. Their bold white "shoulder" patches and white outer tail feathers make them instantly recognizable.

**Above** Goldfinches frequent hedgerows, as well as other open areas, where weeds are plentiful enough to offer an abundance of seeds. They are particularly fond of thistles.

create a bird-free environment used by birds only in winter.

Of course, large areas of hedgerows remain and there are still many areas where the patchwork of fields growing different crops is the major feature of the landscape. But even there, modern methods of hedge maintenance are both unsightly and destructive. Flaying by rotary cutters may be cheap, but the results show an intrinsic lack of

**Left** Magpies are most abundant where open fields are broken by tall, overgrown hedges. Sadly, they are vicious predators of bird eggs and young and destroy many nests of other hedgerow birds, such as the Garden Warbler (**below**), which is bringing food to its young brood.

care for hedgerow and countryside alike. Many farmers, usually using contractors, flay their hedgerows at the wrong time of the year, often when birds are breeding, and probably break the law by disturbing or destroying nests.

**Walking a hedge**

Before walking a hedge, the farmer's permission should be obtained and care should be taken not to damage crops. Hedgerows are at their best in late spring when birds are singing and all the summer visitors have arrived. As the hedge is walked, bird after bird will be flushed and fly a few metres before diving into cover once more. Eventually the individual will arrive at the end of its territory and the nest flush will send it back overhead, or in a loop out over the field.

# FORESTS: DECIDUOUS

**Left** Mixed oak woods, such as this one at St. Cloud near Paris, are frequently full of birds from a wide variety of species.

**Below** A Nuthatch approaches its tree hole nest in a birch. These birds always reduce the size of the entrance hole with mud, whether it is necessary or not.

Woodland is one of the richest of all bird habitats and everywhere it is being destroyed. In cases like the great forests of the Amazon basin, the very existence of the planet may be at stake. Elsewhere, in temperate lands, invaluable wildlife refuges may be lost for ever. Forests cannot be created overnight. They are a complex habitat that lives by its own rules of growth, death and regeneration. At their climax of maturity, forests offer a home to the widest variety of different species of birds and other wildlife. The dominant trees are several hundred years old and their sheer size creates a shadow where little else can grow. Then they die and, in crashing to the gound, an open space is created where light can penetrate and where a whole new bloom of life can flourish.

### The new woodlands

A timber shortage has, in many areas of Britain, led to a policy of replanting woodland, with government encouragement and long term tax advantages. Sadly, this has resulted in a rash of new forests of a single species such as "foreign"

deciduous trees to hide the monstrosities. No doubt there are birds that are grateful for small mercies, but many species need extensive forests of native trees and these habitats are becoming decidedly rare.

### Essential forest homes

Birds of prey, Owls, and the bigger Woodpeckers all need large mature forests where they can breed without disturbance. Yet, just as these species have their own individual requirements, so do other birds need younger forests, forest clearings, forest edges and even flooded and burnt-over forests. Some birds need particular trees to be dominant, either for food or because the trees are an integral part of a particular niche. Others may need dead or dying trees for similar reasons. Others still may need a particular mixture of trees, like the European Black Woodpecker which inhabits mature conifer forests, but prefers to excavate its nest in old beech trees.

By destroying the variety of forests and by planting closely ranked foreign species as replacements, we have deprived many species of their homes. Some have been able to adapt, but others have declined and may disappear. The demise of the Ivory-billed Woodpecker in the

**Above** Lesser Spotted Woodpeckers are elusive little birds that excavate their nest holes in dead or dying trees. They spend much of their time feeding among the smallest branches of the canopy.

**Right** The Jay is a typical bird of oak woods that has the squirrel-like habit of burying acorns during the autumn to provide extra food during the short days of winter.

spruce and larch. These are quick-growing trees that do well on poor soils and their planting creates a monoculture quite different to the natural forests they replace. They are also planted on areas that are otherwise incapable of producing anything of economic value, for example on upland bogs and moorland that are valuable to wildlife in their own right.

Such a policy has had disastrous effects on many native species for, with a few notable exceptions, they offer little to birds. Yet these introduced conifers form some of the largest forests in the landscape. Because of criticism, it is now a well-established practice to line the margins of such plantations with a mixture of native

cypress swamps of Florida and Louisiana can be attributed to the destruction and disturbance of their forest homes. Here was a magnificent bird that was protected and watched over, but only when it was too late. So the Ivory-bill followed the Passenger Pigeon and the Carolina Parrakeet on to the extinction list of birds eliminated from North America in a matter of a hundred years. It can happen elsewhere, and doubtless will.

Basically, woodland can be divided into three broad categories: deciduous woods, conifer woods, and mixed woods. Each has a characteristic bird population. Though many species may be shared, the actual numbers of birds – that is their abundance – differ quite considerably from one type to another. In the simplest terms, conifer woods hold Crossbills, which feed on pine seeds, while deciduous woods hold Jays, which feed on acorns. Things are, however, seldom as simple as we would like them to be. The actual species of conifer will determine not only which species of Crossbill will be found, but also the breeding density of a wide variety of other species. Some may dominate in pines, others in larch or spruce. Similarly with deciduous woods, there may be an abundance of one Warbler among oaks and another among beech woods, even though both birds occur in both woods. Even different species of oak will produce different dominant birds.

### Deciduous wood categories
Some of the most intensively studied woodland bird populations are in Britain. Dividing the deciduous woods into four categories – pedunculate oak, sessile oak, beech and birch - we find the Chaffinch the dominant species in all categories. That ubiquitous summer visitor, the Willow Warbler, is the second most abundant bird in pedunculate oak and birch woods, whereas that place is taken by the Pied Flycatcher and the Great Tit in sessile oak and beech woods respectively.

Certainly some species are more or less confined to particular types of deciduous tree. The Pied Flycatcher, which is the second most abundant species in sessile oaks, is actually completely absent from the lists of all three other woodland types. These woods also have Wood Warbler more highly placed than the others, while Redstarts are present in both types of oakwood, but absent from beech and birch woods. The propensity of birds to occupy a particular type of forest cannot be overstressed.

### Chorus of a deciduous forest
Walking a deciduous forest soon after dawn on a spring day, one is exposed to a richness of songs and calls that is unique. The Finches, Warblers, Woodpeckers, Creepers and Nuthatches, the Thrushes and Titmice, may all combine to produce a chorus of song. Individual species will, of course, dominate, but the others are there to be picked out. Scarcer birds may need a bit of searching for, and the predators may prove highly elusive. Searching for the nocturnal Owls is definitely a hit and miss affair during daylight. Yet, if one is lucky enough to locate a daylight roost of an Owl, there is a good chance that it will be found at the same

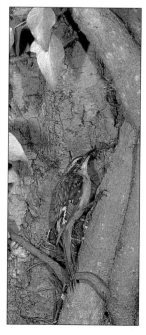

**Far left** The Northern Goshawk is the most fearsome predator of deciduous and mixed forests throughout the northern hemisphere. It is a powerful bird that nests high in a major tree.

**Left** Treecreepers are typical inhabitants of deciduous woodlands and often place their nests behind the loose bark of an old forest tree. They feed among bark crevices on small insects and their eggs.

## Feeding stations

Knowing which birds feed where is often the key to locating them Even in a single tree different species feed at different levels and in different ways.

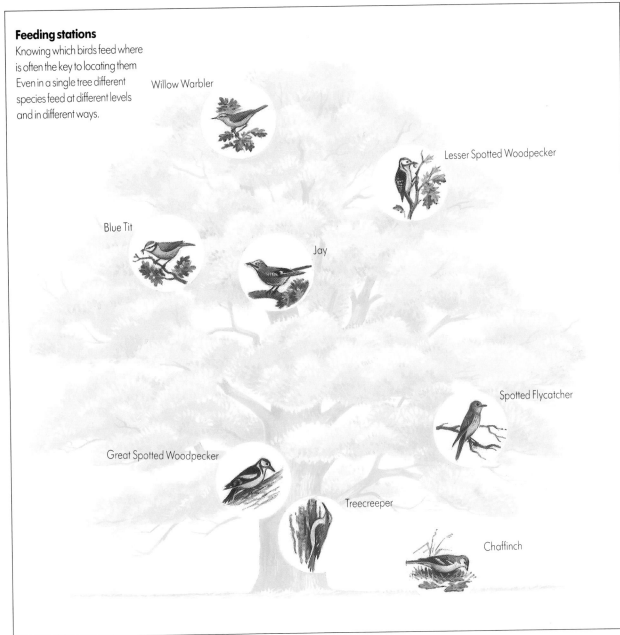

Willow Warbler

Lesser Spotted Woodpecker

Blue Tit

Jay

Spotted Flycatcher

Great Spotted Woodpecker

Treecreeper

Chaffinch

place over and over again, day after day.

Several years ago a friend showed me the roost of a Tawny Owl in a Black Woodpecker's hole deep inside a Belgian forest. The hole was near the top of a broken off tree and only the tail of the Owl could be seen as it roosted, Ostrich-like, with its head and body inside the hole. I returned on two different occasions and at different seasons and each time the Tawny Owl's tail was on view. Even a party of 16 birders did not disturb it in its hideaway.

With the forest-dwelling daytime predators, a completely different approach is required. One can take pot luck, but it is a much better tactic to seek a vantage point outside the forest where good views over the canopy can be obtained. Patience will be rewarded when the raptors start to soar in mid-morning and, in spring and early summer, the displays of species such as Goshawk and Honey Buzzard can be spectacular.

# CONIFEROUS

Outstanding among these are the great Owls - the Great Grey and Hawk Owls, which occur on both sides of the Atlantic, together with the smaller Tengmalm's (Boreal) Owl. In the forests of northern Europe there is also the Ural Owl, the North American equivalent of which is the Barred Owl, which is much more widespread. These Owls breed early in the year, when the ground is still covered with ice and snow.

Northern conifers also have many other species that are not seen elsewhere. In Europe the Capercaillie, a large Turkey-like Grouse, is confined to conifers, while the Black Grouse is seldom found far from their cover. In North America both Spruce and Ruffed Grouse are conifer birds. Of course, the more catholic species are just as at home among conifers as they are in deciduous forests and, in Britain, Chaffinch, Willow Warbler, Robin, and Redstart all figure highly on the list of

**Left** Crested Tits are confined to conifer forests and seldom move more than a mile from where they were reared. They have thus failed to colonize many new Scottish forests from their Speyside stronghold.

**Below** The Capercaillie is the largest of the Grouse and found only in extensive conifer forests, where it lives on a diet of pine needles. Despite being favoured as a game bird, it is said to have a turpentine flavour.

Conifer forests cover huge areas of the Northern Hemisphere between the deciduous forests to the south and the taiga and tundra to the north. Because of short growing seasons and the unyielding nature of much of the underlying geology, these great forests have suffered less than the more temperate, broad-leaved woods to the south. Yet huge areas have been clear-felled for pulp and timber. Fortunately, they are fast-growing, but replanting produces a forest of uniform age that lacks much of the richness of natural woodland. There is also, as we have seen, a passion for planting conifers in areas where they do not naturally occur and this creates another quite distinct type of habitat.

### The great northern forests

It is perhaps everyone's ambition to visit the great northern forests, if only to see a few charismatic birds that are otherwise unlikely to be seen.

most abundant species. Many of the same birds also do well among the plantations of introduced conifers, though here the dominant species tends to be Great Tit, closely followed by Goldcrest. The latter is one of the few species that has really done well as a result of plantations.

Young plantations are fenced off to protect the trees from damage by mammals and the low vegetation and general lack of disturbance creates a secure, heath-like habitat that is perfect for several non-woodland birds. In Britain, Whitethroat and Tree Pipit find these heaths ideal and the numbers and range of the Hen Harrier have increased hand in hand with the extension of planting. As the trees grow, these birds are

**Left** Confined exclusively to conifer forests, the Crossbill feeds on a somewhat monotonous diet of seeds extracted from cones. This bird uses a head of a bullrush as a perch prior to drinking.

**Above** The Hawk Owl is a typical inhabitant of conifer forests, where it perches quite openly during daylight.

replaced by others, but the dark, unthinned plantation is a disappointing habitat for birds.

### Mature forests

In contrast, natural mature forests, with a cross-section of trees of different ages, are full of birds. The 'crests and kinglets are typical conifer feeders, spending much of their time high in the trees and nesting on high outer branches. Their high-pitched calls are often the only indication of their presence. The more distinctive and louder calls of the Titmice and Chickadees are the most obvious of forest sounds. In North America the Black-capped Chickadee is found throughout the forests from southern Alaska to Newfoundland, though it also extends southwards through parts of the Midwest. The Boreal Chickadee has a similar range, while the Mountain Chickadee is confined to the conifer forests of the Rockies. In Europe, Coal and Crested Tits are the most conifer-orientated, though the Siberian Tit is confined to the northern forests and the Great Tit is abundant in more southern conifers.

# MIXED WOODS

With some species confined to deciduous woodland and others to stands of pure conifers, it would be reasonable to assume that mixed forests containing both types of tree would offer the best birding of all. In fact mixed woods are very good, but they do not offer a combination of all the woodland birds of the Northern Hemisphere. Some species require extensive forests of one particular species of tree: if that tree is absent then so is the bird. Once again it depends on the make-up and extent of the forest. Many mixed forests are artificial, the result of planting, often of decorative conifers, during the 19th century. The more exotic conifers were, at that time, treated as something special and confined to parks around stately homes. More widely planted, at least in Britain, was Scot's pine which was used as both wind break and as shelter for Pheasants. These pines were often planted alongside or among existing deciduous woods to create a mixed wood that was allowed to mature quite naturally. Wherever such old woods exist they are excellent in providing a niche for a wide range of species.

Crossbills, 'crests, Tits and other typical conifer birds are perfectly happy provided that there are sufficient trees to meet their requirements. So too are the Jays, Thrushes, Titmice and Finches of deciduous woods. Relatively few birds actually need both types of trees, so the combination is really of greatest benefit to the bird-watcher, who is able to enjoy a greater range of species within a single forest.

**Margins**

Under natural conditions, mixed forests only occur where conifers and deciduous trees meet, that is at the margins, where neither one nor the other has a distinct advantage. Such areas usually involve a mixture of conifers and birch. The latter is never a climax species, being ousted by larger hardwoods such as oak, in maturing deciduous forests. However, it is an excellent colonizer and is able to find a niche among the conifers at the edge of their range and where conditions such as temperature or boggy ground prevent conifers from becoming dominant.

The combination of birch woods and conifers is not only widespread, but also rich in birds. Some of the highest densities of birds such as Chaffinch and Willow Warbler can be found in this natural mixture. It is, of course, a somewhat precarious habitat, for even a slight change in the prevailing conditions can upset the balance and produce a shift towards a deciduous or a conifer climax.

Birch is not the only "marginal" species that can co-exist with conifers. Alders and willows are both capable of colonizing the damp edges of marshes and will, if conditions permit, grow into sizable trees. Inevitably, there are birds that have taken advantage of such natural conditions and while the birch-conifer combination is favoured by, amongst others, Redpolls, the alder-conifer combination is perfectly suited to Siskins. In fact, these are two closely related species which both feed Tit-like by hanging to reach the seeds of their favoured food: yet they are completely different in colouration.

**Below** The Willow Tit inhabits damp and secondary growth woodland. Its harsh nasal calls distinguish it from the similar Marsh Tit, but it is also rather more scruffy than that bird, with a distinctive pale panel in the closed wing, as shown here.

**Above** Sadly declining in Britain, the Wood Lark's particular requirements are met in woodland clearings and heath with short grassy areas where it can feed.

**Right** A male Redstart brings a crane fly to its tree hole nest. These summer visitors may be abundant in the western oak woods of Britain.

### Predators

The predator population of mixed woods differs little from that of either deciduous or conifer forests. Most of the woodland Hawks are quite content to build their nests in whatever large trees are available. Thus the widespread, but scarce, Goshawk is found nesting high in both deciduous and conifer trees. Some species, such as the Osprey and Golden Eagle, would seem to be confined to conifers, but this is surely because these are the trees that are available, rather than because of a distinct preference. Both these large raptors will equally build their nests on cliffs (the Eagle) or on islands (Osprey). In fact, the original British Ospreys were all island-nesters, whereas their modern replacements all build in trees, like the birds of Scandinavia from where they have doubtless derived.

# OPEN COUNTRY: HEATHLAND

Throughout most of the temperate world, natural open country is in short supply. Grasslands, heathlands, scrub and desert are natural open ground, but they have always been limited in extent in Europe.

### Destruction of grassland

The ploughing of grasslands has had a serious effect on many species. In Europe the Great Bustard once roamed across huge areas of the continent where poor soils and climate prevented the growth of forests, and where sheep and poor cattle-grazing were the only possible methods of exploitation. Today this magnificent bird is confined to the plains of Portugal and Spain, to East Germany and to the Hungarian-Danube plains. It is becoming decidedly scarce even there and, unless action is taken, it will disappear from region after region. A similar story can be told of the decline of the Greater and Lesser Prairie Chicken of the United States.

**Above**  Heath fires cause enormous amounts of damage every year. A few are natural, but most are the result of human foolishness. From a bird's viewpoint the result is the same — another area of valuable heathland lost.

**Right**  Stonechats are among the most obvious inhabitants of European heathland. This male has caught an Emperor Moth and perches openly atop a gorse bush before feeding its young in the safety of their well hidden nest.

The main problem with grasslands is that they make wonderful cereal fields, but the same cannot be said of the heathlands. These exist because the underlying geology produces thin and infertile soils. They support sparse grasses together with a few hardy shrubs that seldom, if ever, grow to any height. Once, as in the case of the Mediterranean *maquis* they may have held poor woodland, but man and his browsing goats have largely destroyed the trees and only thorny evergreens have been able to survive.

Modern farming techniques, coupled with agricultural subsidies, have put even these areas under pressure. In northern regions, heathland has been cleared, ploughed and fertilized into producing crops. Stony fields are now producing cereals and carrots where once the gorse held Dartford Warblers, Stonechats and Red-backed Shrikes. Without chemicals and subsidies they would revert to heath or perhaps to scrub.

## Heathland

Heathland is a dynamic habitat which is always under threat. If left alone it will gradually become

overgrown. Clumps of gorse and thorn will provide shelter for trees such as birch to gain a foothold and this leads inevitably to woodland - no matter how poor. Such changes will alter the bird population, so that creating and controlling heathland is an essential part of maintaining the diversity of birds in any area.

Despite public appeals via the media, heaths are particularly prone to fire, and every summer blazes destroy hundreds of hectares of vegetation. Sadly, many birds and their nests are destroyed,

**Left** A Dartford Warbler may find a young conifer a perfect song post, but as these introduced trees mature the Warbler loses another piece of the heathland on which it depends for its existence.

**Above** Great Grey Shrikes are found among open uncultivated land where they frequently perch quite openly. This bird has caught a mouse and impaled it on its thorny larder.

but being only a phase in regeneration, fires may actually benefit the maintenance of heathland. It would, of course, be less dramatic to maintain them with grazing stock, as happens on several nature reserves.

Watching birds on heathland requires nothing but a quick eye and instant reactions. Many of the more interesting birds of low vegetation are confirmed skulkers that make a sudden appearance only to disappear into the next patch of cover. The Dartford Warbler is typical of the breed, but all the Mediterranean Warblers are self-effacing to a greater or lesser extent. This is in contrast to the Chats that inhabit the same areas. Whinchat and Stonechat are both prominent perchers that pounce Shrike-like on their prey and, in many areas, are the most obvious birds.

# SCRUBLAND

Wherever land is neglected it is quickly colonized by a wide variety of vegetation. Typical invading shrubs are hawthorn, elder and hazel, which can, in a relatively short space of time, convert an area of open ground into an impenetrable thicket. Brambles and gorse often act as shelter to these shrubs but they, in turn, provide shelter for young oaks and beeches on the route towards becoming a forest. Scrub is, then, a temporary phase in the vegetation cycle. Under natural conditions this habitat must have been confined to areas that had been cleared by a natural disaster. Today most disasters are man made and scrub moves in when a change of policy leads to neglect, or when some other folly occurs.

**Above** A female Yellowhammer feeds its wellgrown brood in its gorse sited nest. These are typical scrubland birds that have adapted to the similar landscape of hedgerows.

**Left** Red-backed Shrikes have suffered a serious decline in Britain. They frequent scrubland and heaths, but are also found along hedgerows and in orchards.

## Rabbits and grassland

In the 1950s farmers introduced the disease of myxomatosis to Britain in an effort to control the number of rabbits. The practice, despite its obnoxious character, was a success and the population of these fast-breeding mammals was decimated. As a direct result the number of Buzzards crashed dramatically - rabbits were, in many areas, this bird's staple food. What concerns us here, however, is the effect that the demise of the rabbit had on scrubland. Areas such as the chalk downland of southern England, which were formerly maintained as short-cropped grass by the rabbits, were quickly converted to scrub by invading (unchecked) gorse, thorn and elder. Sheep are good at maintaining grassland, but rabbits are much better.

Scrub is a fine bird habitat, but open heathland with short-cropped grass is much rarer and so in greater need of conservation. Birds such as the Wood Lark, Red-backed Shrike and Nightjar are all linked to open rather than scrub-covered ground. All are sadly in decline as the heaths disappear under the plough, or are converted to scrub.

## Havens for breeding

Scrub forms dense thickets that provide many species with a safe haven in which to breed. In southern England, good dense thickets are often occupied by Nightingales, magnificent songsters but decidedly skulking birds. Whitethroat and Lesser Whitethroat, Linnet, Goldfinch, Wren and Blackbird all nest in thickets as do Long-tailed Tits. In winter these same thickets offer a safe roost to flocks of Finches and Thrushes, while in the autumn the crop of berries is essential to departing Warblers as they seek to put on fat for the long journey to come.

Perhaps one bird above all others is identified with scrubland, for Yellowhammers are seldom far from dense thickets. These colourful buntings perch openly to proclaim their territories and utter their characteristic jingling song. They construct a neat cup of grasses, usually lined with hair, at the foot of a shrub well away from prying eyes. The three to five eggs are incubated by the less colourful female, who may be fed by her boldly coloured mate. Yellowhammers regularly

**Above** The Lesser Whitethroat prefers low scrub-like vegetation, often along woodland margins. Its rattling song resembles that of a Yellowhammer, but without the final flourish.

rear two or three broods each season.

In some areas scrub is virtually the only substantial vegetation that can survive. On offshore islands and on windy headlands, all vegetation is pruned by the wind and grows to only a metre or so in height. In many places, patches of scrub are the only cover available to birds, and during migration seasons they offer a home to all manner of small migrants. Such headlands and islands often become migration watch points and a thorough searching of scrub is a regular part of the daily routine at all bird observatories. Where scrub is thin on the ground, an isolated patch of cover may acquire a reputation as the resort of all manner of rarities.

# SANDY WASTES

Sandy and stony wastes are decidedly scarce in Britain, unusual in Europe and localized in North America. In Britain, most are confined to the coasts where the sea has built up a succession of beaches to create a shingly waste such as that at Dungeness in Kent. Once the Breckland of East Anglia was no more than stony ground with a sparse covering of poor grasses. These bare, closely cropped areas provided ideal breeding grounds for Stone-curlew and Wheatear, both of which have since declined as these areas have changed.

On the continent of Europe, such conditions exist along the coast, but also inland where infertile sands are used for grazing sheep and goats. One very special place is the stony wasteland of La Crau, which is effectively the youthful delta of the River Durance, in Provence, France. Here is a plain of stones with only the thinnest covering of grass. It is unique in being the only place in Europe outside Iberia to hold Sandgrouse.

## North American wastes

North America has its sandy and stony wastes in plenty, even if they are mainly localized in the south-west. In fact the states of Nevada and New Mexico have a semi-desert landscape that simply does not exist in Europe. Here broken rocky areas are mixed with sandy plains, dried out salt-lakes and dune systems. Vegetation varies from a few scanty grasses to dense bushes of aromatic herbs. The rolling sage brush of the Western movies is typical of these dry, desolate wastes. Here too are cactus, thorny shrubs and masses of flowers when the erratic rain eventually falls. Yet despite its apparent hostility, a wide range of birds have managed to adapt to this arid landscape. Most notable is perhaps the extraordinary Roadrunner – a giant Cuckoo - but there are Cactus Wrens, Curve-

**Below** Pin-tailed Sandgrouse inhabit the dry sandy wastes of southern Europe, where they are most often seen flighting to drinking water. This male guards its recently hatched youngster.

**Left** Stone-curlews find it increasingly difficult to live alongside agriculture as the sandy wastes they prefer disappear under the plough.

**Above** Wheatears inhabit a range of open uncultivated country including sandy wastes. This male brings food to its young hidden deep in a rocky cleft, but these birds will also nest in rabbit burrows.

billed, Thrashers, Scaled and Harlequin Quails, plus various Sparrows, Juncos and the delightful little Elf Owl which nests in holes in the giant saquaro cactus.

### European sandy wastes

While the deserts and semi-deserts of North America seem relatively safe from development, the same, alas, cannot be said of the sandy wastes of Europe. Virtually throughout the continent, they are subject to reafforestation on a large scale, with alien eucalyptus. The coastal wastelands face other threats from either military or tourist development. Low flat land is at a premium in many regions and, in coastal areas, is often regarded as ideal for airfields for both military and commercial use. La Crau in France and Dungeness in England have both been used for airfields, while the Breckland is a veritable kaleidoscope of military air bases of one sort or another.

Coastal areas are also threatened with direct tourist development, with hotels and apartments that rise virtually overnight from shingly and sandy wastes where only a short time before there were Stone-curlews, Wheatears, Larks and Hoopoes. Even areas spared from direct development may be covered with polythene to produce the vegetables that the vast summer population demands. In southern Crete the area of polythene extends like a huge shimmering lake over an area that only a short time ago held a few hungry sheep, while in Almeria in Mediterranean Spain there is so much polythene that figures of thousands of hectares have been quoted. Inside the plastic hot-houses, everything is reared in "grow bags" - artificial farming at its best.

Watching birds over the sandy and stony wastes that do remain is largely a matter of scan and see. There are no hot-spots that act as centres, and exploration must needs be a sampling rather than a thorough search. A looping walk out and back may produce nothing at one spot and hosts of birds at another. What is certain is that such areas contain certain birds that are seldom or never seen elsewhere.

# HILLS AND MOUNTAINS: PEAKS AND BUTTRESSES

Hills and mountains are among the last untouched wilderness left on Earth, though the modern ski-tourist industry seems intent on not leaving a single decent slope untouched longer than necessary. Neverthless, the uplands are often a refuge for birds that were once more widespread, even in the lowlands. The birds of prey are classic examples of species that have been eliminated from most of their lowland range and are making a last stand among the mountains.

**High mountain birds**

Watching true mountain birds has always been both a great pleasure and something to indulge in while young. To reach the higher slopes or tops requires a stout pair of boots and a stout heart, as well as sensible precautions in terms of protective clothing, food and navigational aids. Hill-walking is

**Left** Meadow Pipits are among the most widespread birds of open ground. They nest from sea level to the slopes of high mountains, where they are often the most numerous bird.

**Above** Golden Eagles frequently nest in trees, but are more typically birds of mountain buttresses where they will use the same nest site for many years.

certainly not an activity to be undertaken lightly, yet the rewards are birds that are never or only seldom seen elsewhere. Though it is easy to attack ski-tourist developments, it has to be said just how much birders have come to appreciate the ease of access to the high slopes they provide. Cable cars are excellent leg-savers, and for the mature bird-watcher they offer the only route to many species. They should not, however, lull one into believing that mountains are anything but dangerous to the ill-prepared.

High mountains are home to species like (Rock) Ptarmigan, Wallcreeper, Lammergeier, Snow Finch and Alpine Accentor that cannot be seen reliably

elsewhere. To watch these birds one must reach the tops, or at least the highest slopes. They are joined in summer by birds such as Snow Bunting and Dotterel that are more typically tundra-breeders, but which find that mountain tops well to the south bear an acceptable resemblance to the lands beyond the Arctic Circle. Finally there are birds that, though more widespread, find a refuge among mountains.

In Europe the latter include Golden Eagle as well as Imperial, Short-toed and Bonelli's Eagles, all of which are more at home among the foothills. In fact, it is difficult to be optimistic about the future

**Above** Choughs are in their element wherever windy conditions prevail and where they can feed on short-cropped grass. Their aerial mastery is often quite spectacular.

**Right** Shore Larks are frequently found in the tundra, though they also frequent mountains and grasslands as well as shorelines.

of European birds of prey, as numbers continue to decline throughout their range and irrespective of species. For all of these birds, the hills and mountains may represent a last stand, rather than a last stronghold.

Food is not particularly abundant in mountain areas: indeed it is mainly relatively safe breeding grounds that bring many birds to these regions. Rocky buttresses are favoured by many species and bird-watchers intent on finding nesting sites should remember their "nest boxes" and search buttresses and cliffs facing away from direct sunlight and the prevailing wind. Gorges often provide shelter from several directions and are widely used by Eagles. Most birds of prey avoid the major peaks, preferring instead the lower and thus more accessible cliffs.

These same buttresses are also preferred by the Choughs, whose aerial mastery is so complete that they virtually "play" in the air. Here too are Peregrines, Jackdaws and Ravens, though all three are capable of breeding quite happily at sea level if they can find the right conditions, and even on buildings in some instances.

Few mountain birds are as tough as the Ptarmigan, which make their summer home among the highest plateaux and slopes. During the breeding season they are clothed in a camouflage of greys, but in winter they become completely white to blend with the snowy wastes. Somehow they eke out a living in the snow, often burying themselves in drifting snow as an insulation against bitter cold and biting winds. They may descend two or three hundred metres at this time, but seldom, if ever, to the valley floor.

# SCREES AND ROCKS

Comparatively few birds live among the towering peaks of major mountain systems and even fewer are confined to particularly high altitudes. For most species the right habitat is the right place to be and, if the right habitat is found only at altitude, then altitude becomes an essential ingredient in their lifestyle. Thus "mountain" birds such as Ptarmigan, Dotterel, Snow Bunting and Chough all breed at sea level where conditions are right. For the Snow Bunting and Ptarmigan such conditions are found beyond the Arctic Circle. For the Dotterel too this is the norm, though these attractive little Plovers did breed for a few years below sea level on the reclaimed polders of Holland. In contrast, the Chough is able to find suitable habitats along cliff-girt coastlines at the same (or even lower) lattitudes that it breeds at in the mountains. Thus it can be argued that these four widespread European birds are not really "mountain" birds at all.

**Below** Open scree provides the ideal breeding site for the Lapland Bunting, which constructs its nest in a crevice between the rocks.

**Bottom** In summer Snow Buntings inhabit high mountain plateaux, while in winter they are most abundant along bare beaches and coastal marshes.

**Left** Ptarmigan are widespread in the tundra as well as on high mountain tops farther south. This bird is in the grey plumage of summer.

**Above** A winter plumage Ptarmigan merges well with the snow-covered slopes that it inhabits for much of the year.

The Alpine Accentor, Wall Creeper and Snow Finch, however, are mountain birds, with ranges that are restricted to the highest regions of Europe. None can be found at sea level on the tundra, and none can exist away from sheer cliffs or bare rocky wastes. Occasionally the delightful Wall Creeper may wander and it does, more or less regularly, visit valley churches to climb their spires in winter. But the majority of birds are confined to the sheer cliff faces of mountains.

**Refugees from the lowlands**
Many more birds find the hills a refuge, a place where they can exist without disturbance. Over huge areas of lowland, woodland has been cleared for agriculture and reafforestation schemes offer only an alien version of what previously existed. In many mountain districts, extensive natural forests remain, either because they are difficult to work, or are unsuitable for timber, or by virtue of the protection granted to a water catchment area, or some such. These woods provide homes to birds that once bred in lowland forests wherever they

existed. Sparrowhawk, Goshawk, Booted Eagle and Eurasian Black Vulture are all birds that find strongholds in hilly areas, but that are well capable of occupying lowland forests. These persecuted birds of prey also have their equivalents among the small birds. Both Meadow Pipit and Sky Lark are found among the hills, even among the high screes of sliding stones, yet both are also found breeding at sea level. Had Pipit and Lark been persecuted like the birds of prey, we might well regard them too as typical mountain birds.

**Citril Finch**
One of the most specialized of mountain birds is the Citril Finch. This relative of the Canary and more widespread Serin has a particular niche above the tree line where the pines and firs start to thin out and give way to dwarf forms of Alpine vegetation. Here the Citril sings and nests among the stunted and scattered trees. It is, of course, a niche that also exists in the taiga, where latitude rather than altitude has a similar effect on thinning out the conifers. Interestingly neither the Citril Finch nor any other small Finch has made this niche totally its own.

137

# BOGS AND MOORS

In general, mountains receive more than their fair share of rain and, even on the Equator, much of this falls as snow. Long before their valleys were dammed, mountains were already acting as storage reservoirs for the lowlands. Cold winters, often with temperatures well below freezing for weeks at a time, are characteristic of mountains and the higher than average precipitation falls as snow and is stored until temperatures rise in the spring. This abundance of water has, over the centuries, created bogs where little but moss can grow. These, in turn, hold water which creates more bogs and a tough landscape of peat and water. The melt of snow in spring saturates the more gently shelving slopes, fills the bogs and lakes and is only slowly released into the rivers. This is a major safety check, for fast-rising spate rivers are both dangerous and wasteful of water. The quaking bogs of peat and moss that are so

**Left** A Greenshank settles on its nest in the boggy moorland where it breeds. These are long distance migrants that spend the winter on marshes thousands of miles to the south.

**Above** The Hen Harrier frequents open moorland with bogs and marshes, where it is a major predator on small birds. The planting of uplands with young conifers offers secure breeding sites and has enabled the Harrier to increase.

characteristic of many hilly districts, offer tundra-like conditions to many birds, some of which would otherwise be found only hundreds of kilometres to the north.

## Waders

The number of waders on these damp moorlands is often surprisingly high, with Dunlin, Golden Plover and Curlew being quite numerous among the hills of northern Britain. In Scotland these

species are joined by Greenshank, Whimbrel and a handful of species that can just, but only just, find a foothold here. Recent years have seen several predominantly Scandinavian birds colonize the northern British moors. Temminck's Stint, Wood Sandpiper and Purple Sandpiper have established breeding populations, to join the Red-necked Phalarope which already nested. All these birds use the wild bogs of the Scottish hills, but others such as the Lapland Bunting and Shore Lark, have colonized without being dependent on these tundra-like marshes.

Moorland is also used by Grouse, and by their special predator, the Golden Eagle. To watch an Eagle quarter a hillside, gliding apparently lazily over a ridge, turn a blind corner and surprise a Grouse, is both impressive and fortunate. It is also somewhat annoying for the gamekeeper and the sportsman. Though Grouse are hunted wherever they occur, it is only in Britain that their pursuit has been converted into a ritual. The Grouse here is the Red Grouse, a sub-species of the widespread Willow Grouse, or Willow Ptarmigan.

## Moorland predators

Grouse moors are carefully managed to produce the maximum population of Red Grouse ready for the shooting season to open on 12 August. Areas are regularly burned over on a rota system to produce the first young shoots of heather that a healthy population of Grouse require. Males establish territories over the moor and defend their domains against intruders. Young birds that are unable to obtain a territory are destined to a gypsy-like existence of moving through the territories of others, or of occupying marginal territory of rough grass with little heather. Sportsmen regularly argue that these "spare" birds are destined to die and that it is this surplus that they shoot.

While there is much to support the "surplus theory", it is not clear that only "spare" birds are actually shot. Old males and females get shot as well and it is these birds, with their superior experience, that are most likely to survive natural hazards to breed the following year.

These moors are patrolled by several predators other than man. The hillsides may hold Golden Eagles, which most landowners now regard with pride rather than hatred. Here too are Merlins with their eyes on smaller prey, such as Meadow Pipit or Sky Lark. And, in the lower bogs and moors, there are Hen Harriers, often regarded as the enemy of young Grouse. It is easy to explain to a sportsman, or his 'keeper, that it is the number of prey that determine the number of predators and not the other way round. But science makes little difference to his aim as he splatters another Harrier and saves a few more chicks to shoot in August. Harriers are protected by law, but their ultimate wellbeing depends on an appreciation of their qualities, rather than on their abilities as Grouse predators.

**Left** The Arctic Skua spends most of its year harrying Gulls and Terns at sea. In summer it switches to the tundra and is largely dependent on lemmings for food.

# FROM BIRDER TO ORNITHOLOGIST: ETHOLOGY

**Above** According to James Fisher an increase in fish waste and decrease in persecution may be behind the establishment of new Fulmar colonies along many coasts.

**Right** The Song Sparrow was the subject of an in-depth study by Mrs M.M. Nice that set the style for all the behavioural monographs that followed.

At first we are content to identify the birds we see, to watch and enjoy them and become familiar with their everyday lives. Gradually we seek to know more. We dip into books, subscribe to magazines and journals, attend lectures, join societies and clubs - but most of all we begin to watch birds in a different way. Our watching becomes purposeful. Of course, such watching needs a background in ornithology to understand what things to look for, but an intensive course of reading together with regular field trips in the company of other bird-watchers soon gets most of us going on research of some sort.

Research is a formidable word. It smacks of sterilized laboratories and has a musty, old book smell to it. In many areas of knowledge, such as physics and chemistry, research is the preserve of white-coated PhD's backed by the resources of universities or international companies. With birds it is different. If a bird-watcher wants to study some aspect of the lives of birds, he can just go ahead and do so. Many of the most important elements of birds' lives have been described by amateurs working on their own. A teacher called David Lack could not stop looking out of his classroom window to watch the colour-ringed Robins that haunted the school grounds. The result was the classic, *The Life of the Robin*, and David Lack became director of a famous ornithological institution, the Edward Grey Institute in Oxford. While there may now be more professional ornithologists than in Lack's day, there are still more birds than there are professionals to cover them. Thus research is full of possibilities for amateurs to make contributions in a positive and meaningful way.

Research may be individual or organized, and may consist of field work or museum and library study. Some types of research lend themselves to field work - the study of breeding behaviour, for

example - whereas others concerned, let us say, with the distribution of a species, are essentially researches through published material. It is just not possible to learn where a bird is found by searching for it: one must rely to a large extent on the efforts of others. But this does not make such research unproductive. There are untold amounts of information buried in miscellaneous journals which could be collated and published, but ornithologists seldom seem to have the time or money to do so.

## Bird psychology

Ethology, the study of animal behaviour, is often thought of as the preserve of the psychologist. It is not. Bird behaviour can be watched and noted by

**Above** German ethologist Konrad Lorenz imprinted Greylag goslings, as their surrogate parent, thus gaining insight into a hitherto unknown area of animal behaviour.

**Below** The European Robin proved the ideal subject for a youthful David Lack to study in depth and produce a classic bird book. Work on common birds produces faster results than studies of rare or elusive species.

anyone with eyes to see. Edmund Selous produced some of the most important bird books published this century, summarizing his observations of many common European species. Anyone who would follow in his steps should read his books. Indeed, to study bird behaviour it is necessary to read what others have achieved before you if you want to do anything of any significance. But it most definitely is not necessary to have reached degree standard.

If bird behaviour interests you, study it. Watch carefully and record exactly what you see. Omit nothing, for the very detail that you require may only be apparent in retrospect. Try to record as much as possible, for too much data is certainly better than too little.

Ethology benefits most from work on birds that are common and easy to watch near the observer's home. Indeed, seabirds are the best

subjects for case studies simply because large numbers are concentrated in small, easy-to-work locations, and because they are generally easy to see and comparatively tame. The observer can watch a great many individuals in a very short space of time. So never try to study the behaviour of a rare or elusive species when a common and tame one would do as well.

# CENSUSES

If the study of bird behaviour is essentially an individual activity, inquiries into distribution are clearly cooperative affairs. In Britain the British Trust for Ornithology (BTO) organized the field work and production of an *Atlas of Breeding Birds*, an idea that has been taken up in many other parts of Europe. The success and popularity of this venture prompted the BTO to follow with a winter atlas project and it presently plans a repeat of the breeding atlas.

**The great bird count**
Based on the National Grid 10km squares, into which Britain is divided, bird-watchers volunteered to search systematically for breeding birds in the square nearest their home over a period of several years. The result has been an incredible increase in our knowledge of birds in Britain. It was the element of competition, with one's own record as much as with others, perhaps, that made for such success. There was always the

chance of another bird, new for the square, to be found in a seldom-visited part of the allotted zone. As a consequence, habitats were searched that had not been visited by ornithologists before; for bird-watchers tend to concentrate at those places that are acknowledged as productive. Spotted Crakes, formerly considered as very rare and irregular breeders, but ones that are so easy to overlook, were found here and there throughout southern England. Other easy-to-miss species were also found to be much more widespread than had been appreciated before.

Operation Seafarer, organized by the Seabird Group, was an attempt to count all British and Irish seabirds so as to provide a base for monitoring the populations of these much-

**Below** By making six visits to an area and plotting the position of each singing Robin on each occasion, an ornithologist is able to build up a picture of the total number of singing males and, therefore, of the number of breeding pairs.

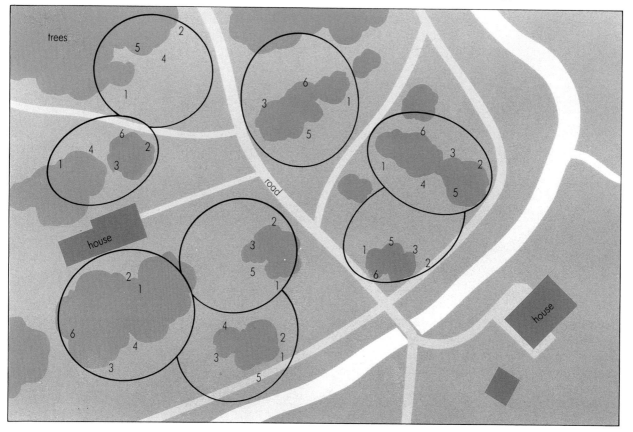

**Left** Counts of seabirds, such as the Gannets on Scotland's Bass Rock, enable ornithologists to monitor the populations of these highly gregarious birds.

**Below** The distribution of Gannets, evenly spaced across the rock, indicates that each bird is on its nest. Non-nesting birds are spaced irregularly.

threatened species. Almost every kilometre of seashore was covered and every cliff and stack examined. Some species, because of the nature of their lives, proved impossible. Others could be no more than sampled. But for a majority of seabirds we now have a good idea of how many there were in 1970-2. This now acts as a yardstick against which changes in population can be measured. Population censuses such as this last for a specific period and are then complete. Doubtless they will be repeated from time to time, perhaps every 10 years or so. Other investigations are open-ended. One of the most important of these is the Common Bird Census of the BTO.

Because of the use to which we wish to put any information gleaned on bird populations, there is actually no need to count all the birds. We want to keep an eye on populations so that if there is a sudden drop or boom we can note it quickly, investigate and perhaps do something about it.

The whole thing really started back in the 1950s when many watchers noted declines in the numbers of what had been, until then, quite common birds. Gradually the decline began to be linked with the use of agricultural chemicals used as insecticides and seed dressings (the

chlorinated hydrocarbons). These persistent chemicals eventually found their way into the body tissue of birds of prey: there was a catastrophic decline in the number of Peregrines. As a result effective preventive measures were taken just in time. It was nearly too late for the Peregrine.

Frightened that they had not known about the effects of change on bird populations, and anxious that a similar disaster should be recognized earlier, the BTO introduced the Common Bird Census to monitor changes in the population of commonplace birds.

**Above** Shot to extinction in Britain last century, the Osprey has recolonized Scotland and now enjoys the sympathy of the public and the tolerance of fishermen.

**Right** Peregrines were one of the primary victims of pesticide poisoning during the 1960s. They are still absent from huge areas of their former range.

In the common bird census system, an area of 40 hectares or so of farm or woodland is selected and visited by an observer five or more times during the peak of spring activity. On each visit the exact position of each singing male bird is plotted on a map. At the end of the season, when all the summer migrants, and the resident birds, have settled down to breed, the maps for each visit are laid over one another and a single map drawn of the completed season's work. From this it is possible to see that the various individual birds have maintained their territories, for records of singing males in different months form clusters in the final map. These clusters are counted and the number of singing males of each species totalled for the year.

While the Common Bird Census does not count every bird, it does give an accurate idea of whether a particular species is doing well or not. CBC workers are scattered throughout the country covering every type of habitat. Some have been covering the same area for 10 or more years and have enjoyed every moment of their constructive field work as well as the fascination of compiling maps and drawing together the final results.

## Building up a picture

When a picture for the whole country emerges, we can see the remarkable recovery that birds can make after an exceptionally hard winter has decimated their numbers. When observatories reported fewer Whitethroats in spring, CBC workers were asked to forward their results for the species as a matter of urgency. Within a few weeks it was apparent that there had been a disaster - the numbers of breeding Whitethroats had suffered a catastrophic decline. Looking for a cause soon revealed that the wintering grounds of this attractive little warbler had suffered a major drought. Soon newspapers and other media were full of stories of human famine in the same area, the Sahel region south of the Sahara Desert. Pictures and film of starving people, and of children in particular, caught the conscience of the western world and led to massive fund raising events such as Band Aid, Live Aid and so on. Yet the work of amateur bird-watchers could have been used to draw attention to the drought months before it hit the headlines and much suffering could have been avoided.

The populations of birds can, then, be monitored in various different ways. Widespread and common birds can be sampled. Birds that are concentrated at a few major sites to breed can be counted, but so too can birds that, while they may breed scattered over huge areas, concentrate into well-defined areas at other times of the year.

Wildfowl are particularly concentrated during the winter and with several species of Geese it is possible to count the complete world total. There are, for example, some 75,000 Barnacle Geese in the world with three quite distinct populations wintering in northwestern Europe. Fluctuations in numbers, as well as the percentage of young birds in the flocks, can tell us which population has enjoyed a good breeding season and which a poor one. We can counter the arguments of sportsmen and farmers who wish to hunt the Geese and we are always alert to disaster.

Censusing birds provides one of the most valuable tools a conservationist can have; it is primary research, often by amateurs, that provides the basis.

**Right** Barnacle Geese, once in serious decline due to overshooting, have responded to protection and increased dramatically during the past 30 years. Their concentration at a few major wintering sites makes them particularly prone to disturbance.

# BANDING AND RINGING

The study of birds by individually marking them with rings is comparatively recent. Yet in the space of 70 years it has led to a complete revolution in our understanding of their lives. Migrant birds have been proved to fly vast distances to and from regular summer and winter homes and even to stop off at the same places along the way. Such facts are well known, and accepted as the major results of ringing, but we gain much other information besides. We know exactly how long an individual wild bird lives. We can estimate the population of a species by comparing the rate at which ringed birds are retrapped in a particular area with the overall chances of retrapping. We take advantage of handling a bird to measure it, note its state of moult and weigh it. If, as often happens, the same bird is retrapped in the same area, then the same measurements can tell us whether or not the bird is gaining weight and how far it has progressed with its moult in a specific period of time. We can find out how old a bird is when it first starts to breed and much more besides.

Taking wild birds for ringing requires a licence from government, and almost all ringers meet the stringent qualifications required and hold a permit from the national ringing scheme. Would-be ringers must be trained by existing ringers and serve a sort of apprenticeship. They must learn how to catch birds safely, how to handle them, how to put rings on and keep accurate records. They must learn the rules and regulations concerning what birds they may or may not ring. So the starting point is to contact a local ringer or visit a bird observatory.

**Above** Mallard, caught by cannon-netting are transferred to holding pens prior to being ringed in South Dakota.

**Left** Heligoland traps, like this one on the island of Lundy, England, are simply giant wire-netting funnels placed over suitable cover to trap migrant birds for ringing.

## Mist nets

Today most birds are caught in mist nets - fine black terylene nets that disappear when suspended against a dark background. These nets must be carefully sited (they can catch cows and people too) and visited every 15 minutes or so. Birds fly into a mist net and drop into a pocket of netting below a shelf-string. There the majority lie still until they are extracted by the ringer - not a job for the clumsy or quick-tempered. Some

**Below** Ringing Manx Shearwaters has proved one of the most productive forms of migration study. Individuals transferred from Britain to the U S. have returned to their nests in a matter of days.

**Right** This Trumpeter Swan is being returned to the water at Red Rock Wildlife Refuge, Montana, with a colourful neck band boldly coded so that it can be read without recatching the bird.

species, notably Tits and Starlings, fight furiously to escape, grabbing footfuls of netting from all directions. The longer they are left, the longer they take to extract. Sometimes a Tit will tie itself in a virtual ball of netting and pose a considerable problem for the ringer. In extreme cases, the ringer must be prepared to cut his net to extricate a bird.

A trapped bird is marked with a light alloy band placed around the tarsus. This is stamped with a serial number and the words INFORM BRITISH MUSEUM (NAT. HIST.) LONDON SW7, which is the clearing address for the British ringing scheme. Reports on, and rings recovered from, dead birds should be sent to the Ringing Officer, BTO, Beech Grove, Tring, Herts. In return the finder receives details of where the bird was ringed and the distance it has travelled.

Despite expressed fears, ringing, when carried out by an expert, does no harm to the bird. If it did, the whole point of it would be destroyed, for the aim of ringing is to study the normal behaviour of normal birds. Accidents do happen, but they are very few indeed, and the gains in knowledge far outweigh the tiny element of risk. In fact, ringing is now regarded as a primary element in conservation work and many bird organizations actively pursue programmes of ringing in their efforts to monitor populations and protect birds in the crucial aspects of their lives. There is clearly little point in spending scarce resources on protecting a bird on its breeding grounds if the greatest danger lies thousands of miles away in its winter quarters.

### The value of ringing

At one time ringers simply ringed; but now they take full advantage of their opportunities to extract the maximum amount of data from the living bird in the hand. Weighing is particularly important. During the day a bird's weight varies considerably, but prior to migrating birds put on fuel in the form of body fat. Some species may double their weight in this way. From weights it is possible to work out a bird's potential range, that is how far it can fly without "refuelling".

Ringing, then, is a powerful weapon in the hands of ornithologists and conservationists, but it is also a fine field sport. With the happy decline of shooting for collections and oology (egg-collecting), other more acceptable activities have taken their place. The hunting instinct, if that's what it is, is now channelled into twitching, ringing and photography - all of which demand skill and craft to reach the required standards.

A great deal of what we know about the lives of birds is a direct result of ringing. By marking an individual bird in this way we can, via a recovery or by others retrapping the bird, learn where it breeds, where it winters and about the route taken between the two. We may learn something of the speed with which it makes its journeys and of places where it stops-over to feed and recuperate. We have learned, for example, that, although Barn Swallows winter throughout Africa south of the Sahara, British Swallows spend their winter in South Africa, while German Swallows winter in West Africa. We have discovered that, while birds migrate on broad fronts crossing seas and deserts along the way, there is still nevertheless a "migrational divide" in Europe. Some birds move south-west, while others move south-east.

## Building up a map

Most ringing stations and ringing groups build up sufficient recoveries of birds to justify creating a map for particular species. Pinned to the wall of the laboratory or ringing hut, these show not only the destinations of birds, but also their origins and the route between the two.

A map of recoveries of British-ringed White-

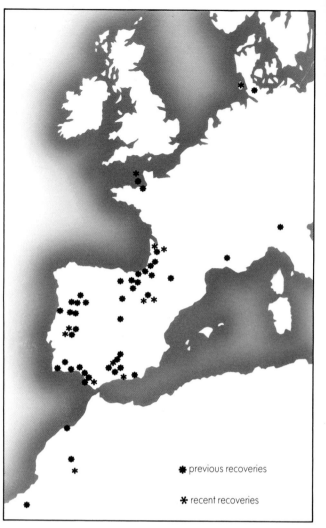

✳ previous recoveries

✱ recent recoveries

**Above** Recoveries of British ringed Robins show a general movement to the southwest, with most recoveries in France, Portugal and Spain.

**Above right** Ringing Ferruginous Hawks in North Dakota produced recoveries that show a general southwards movement, though some wander a little to the north.

**Left** An ornithologist in a field laboratory, or ringing hut, is ringing a Sanderling, one of the long distance migrants that ringers favour.

• recovered during first year of life

• recovered during subsequent years

to-west across the path of birds moving between Europe and Africa. In the Americas the physical barriers run largely north to south, roughly parallel to the routes taken by birds. This has had the effect of concentrating birds into particular "flyways" in North America, whereas European birds have no advantage in concentrating in this way. Such an overview would be impossible without the backing evidence of ringing.

**Below** Ringing young Herring Gulls, like this one, tells us a great deal about the movements of these birds, as well as about their life style and longevity. With birds that are as successful as this species, research is essential to conservation.

**Bottom** Ringing some species, such as this male Blackcap, may be unrewarding from a recovery standpoint, but it does offer ornithologists the opportunity to handle live birds and take weights and measurements.

fronted Geese, for example, tells us that the birds that winter in England come from the population that breeds along the coast of northern Russia and the islands of Novaya Zemlya. But it also shows that these birds do not follow a direct route, but make a loop migration southwards to central Russia on their way westwards to northern Germany, Holland and the Channel coast of France.

A similar map for Knot shows that birds that have been ringed in Britain have actually made a huge transatlantic flight from western Greenland and the Canadian Arctic and that many of these birds continue along the coasts of the southern North Sea and the Atlantic as far as Spain and Morocco. More typical is the map of British ringed Robins, which shows that Robins ringed in Britain move southwestwards to winter in western France and south and west Iberia.

In the Euro-African migration system, most of the significant barriers to bird movement run east-

# MIGRATION STUDIES

It will by now, be apparent to any reader that the author has a particular penchant for the migrations and movements of birds and a fascination with identification. Not surprisingly these two aspects of birding go nicely hand in hand and I am far from being alone in such enthusiasms. Watching migration is, in some instances, as dramatic a spectacle as the wonderful concentrations of birds of prey at Hawk Mountain in Pennsylvania. In Europe we enjoy similar spectacles at the Straits of Gibraltar, the Bosphorus and at Falsterbö in southern Sweden. At Gibraltar and the Bosphorus there are also great spiralling flocks of Storks, though at a different season. These are spectacular migrations that anyone can go and watch - bird movements at their most obvious and dramatic.

Most other birds are less concentrated and their migrations are thus more difficult to detect. We can see birds appear in spring in our gardens and know that they have just arrived. We can watch a flock of birds at a favoured site and know they are migrants because they were not there yesterday. But real dramas are hard to come by and usually require a visit to a special migration watchpoint. In North America there are favoured points along the Gulf Coast and on the northern shores of the Great Lakes. In Europe most migration work has been done in Britain and along the southern shore of the Baltic.

## Migration watch points

Britain boasts a fine network of bird observatories on islands and headlands along its extensive

**Left** This migrant House Martin has become lost after dark and has taken refuge near a lighthouse, doubtless attracted by the beams of light.

**Above** White Storks migrate in large flocks that concentrate into huge, wheeling masses at the narrow sea crossings of Gibraltar and the Bosphorus.

coastline. These are all excellent places to watch migration, to seek out migrants and note the daily comings and goings of a large range of species. Many of these watch points have nearby, or adjacent, lighthouses and it was the birds attracted to the lights that first drew the attention of observatory founders to their potential. Many birds died as a result of flying into the lights, and picking up and identifying the corpses of nocturnal migrants was, at one time, an integral part of the work of observatory enthusiasts. Today, these dangerous structures are fully illuminated so that even dazzled birds can see them and take avoiding action. While most bird observatories are ringing stations, they also attempt to note every bird seen within the observatory area every day. Particular attention is paid to patches of scrub where

**Left** Migrants often get lost when bad weather prevents accurate navigation. This Wheatear has taken refuge on a ship 200 kilometres off the French coast, where it will await better weather before reorientating and continuing its journey.

migrating birds seek shelter. Mostly this is a matter of "doing the rounds" early every morning when birds are most active. Waiting patiently on the sunny and sheltered side of cover is far more effective than thrashing around in the hope of disturbing birds; and it is often surprising what the more patient birder can find. The number of birds will vary day by day and the casual visitor will gain little impression of migration from a single visit.

Just occasionally, particular weather conditions will produce a fall (fall-out) of migrants that it is impossible to ignore. Where there were a few, there can quite suddenly be hundreds or even thousands of birds. Such falls are a dramatic sign of migration that passes largely unseen, but it is every birder's ambition to experience such a fall. Inevitably it is usually the resident wardens at observatories that experience such dramas, together with the few birders who, by sheer good fortune, happen to have chosen that particular day for an outing.

In my early birding days I remember vividly poring over the daily weather forecasts watching for what I thought would be perfect "fall" conditions. What I was seeking was lovely high pressure over Scandinavia in autumn to provide perfect migration weather for nocturnal migrants to set off over the North Sea en masse towards Britain. I then needed a deep depression to arrive in south-eastern England with rain and cloud to force the birds down. Day after day during the peak migration season, the weather system failed to produce the goods. Then suddenly the map predicted everything I wanted. The problem was where to go? The front associated with the depression was predicted to pass through Kent at dawn, and so off I set for Dungeness. I arrived early in pouring rain and had one of those miserable bird-less days that migration seasons can produce. I returned home to be informed that the phone had been ringing all day and that the Suffolk coast had enjoyed the most dramatic fall in history. I'd got the day right, but the front had moved through too fast and the birds had been disorientated over the southern North Sea instead of over Kent.

# CONSERVATION

Being a birder does not inevitably mean that one is a conservationist, in the same way as being a conservationist does not turn one into a birder. Nevertheless, it is difficult to watch birds without being interested in their future and all birders, bird-watchers, twitchers and listers should, at least, be members of their national and/or local bird conservation organization.

### National Organizations

Just as birding is becoming progressively more international, so too is bird conservation. Local conservation societies have local aims, national ones national aims, but birds are the most mobile animals on Earth and their conservation has to be be approached on an international scale. By and large international organizations are low on both funds and muscle, and many of the most important measures are originated by go-ahead "national" organizations. Prime examples are the work of the American Audubon Societies and the British Royal Society for the Protection of Birds. Both organizations are primarily concerned with the birds of their own country, but both recognize the international implications of bird conservation. There are, of course, fully international organizations such as the World Wide Fund for Nature (WWF), the International Council for Bird Preservation (ICBP), and the International Union for the Conservation of Nature (IUCN); but all have great demands on their limited funds and can barely scratch the surface of bird conservation.

### Specialist organizations

There are several more specialized organizations that attempt to deal with specific areas of bird conservation on a world-wide scale. Primary among these is the Wildfowl Trust, the brain-child of Peter Scott, and a model that has shown the way that other organizations could go. The Trust is actively involved in wildfowl conservation throughout the world and its Hawaiian Goose project has been successful in saving, studying and releasing this endangered species back to its native land.

Surprisingly few other specialized organizations have followed the lead shown by the Wildfowl Trust, though it has spawned many imitators

**Above** The Bald Ibis, seen here at one of its few remaining breeding sites at Birecik in Turkey, seems headed for extinction. During 1988 only a single bird was present.

among Duck and Goose enthusiasts. There are, however, organizations that specialize in the conservation of Pheasants, birds of prey, Owls and Cranes. The latter is something of a model of its type and owes its existence to the enthusiasm of two young Americans - George Archibald and the late Ron Sauey. Based in Wisconsin, the International Crane Foundation has a collection that includes every species of this spectacular group of birds. It is active in the study of Cranes and has bridged political boundaries in its conservation work. If anyone has the odd few million (pounds, dollars, deutschmarks or yen) looking for a home, I would recommend it be sent instantly to George.

**Left** The Peregrine captive breeding programme at Jackson Hole, Wyoming, is just one such attempt to restore the Falcon to its previous numbers after the massive 1960s pesticide kill.

**Above** Conservation work takes a variety of forms, but ornithologists are progressively becoming land management, rather than species protection, oriented. Over-grazing, seen on one side of this fence, can ruin perfectly good grassland.

There are other bird groups that have attracted the attention of small bands of enthusiasts for a variety of different reasons. Peregrines have been bred to replace the wild populations wiped out in a number areas by the chemical disasters of the 1960s. In many cases this is, however, no more than enlightened self-interest by keen, perhaps obsessive, falconers. Similarly, there are captive breeding projects devoted to Bustards and backed by enormous funds in the Middle East. Having exterminated their own Bustards as prey for their Falcons, the sheiks are having to look elsewhere for these birds or breed their own. It would be good to know that the vast resources available were to be used for the international conservation of this generally neglected group of birds... but, sadly, I doubt it will.

# CONSERVATION PROJECTS

Conservation projects come in all shapes and sizes. Erecting a garden nest box is as much a bird conservation project as creating a 500-acre reserve. Yet what an individual can do must inevitably be limited when compared to a large and influential organization. Most conservationists agree that if one is really serious then one should own land, for only by doing so can one be certain that it will be reserved and managed for the benefit of birds. Governments, local and state authorities, multinationals and giant corporations, rich and powerful philanthropists can all contribute by using their resources to establish reserves and bird-friendly policies - but what can be done, can also be undone. Land ownership by conservation bodies is the key.

A hundred years ago a nature reserve was an area with a fence around it and notices saying "Keep Out". Today's reserves are actively managed to produce the right conditions for the species most in need of help. Land can be converted to marshes, to swamps, to forests and even be farmed specifically to provide food for wild birds, but it will also be used to educate and enthuse

visitors. Of course if you can begin with an area that is more or less what you want, you start with immense advantages. But even if the newly-acquired reserve is poor, as long as the potentiality is there it can be transformed into what is required.

One of the best examples of this new dynamic approach to bird habitats is to be found at the RSPB's Minsmere Reserve in Suffolk. Here, with the help of the Army and its bulldozers, a series of shallow coastal lagoons have been extended to create "The Scrape", an artificial bird breeding and feeding site of immense importance. The lagoons existed before the Army moved in, and sheltered a few passage waders: the rest is artificial. Islands covered with polythene (to prevent weeds choking them) have been created and the sheeting covered with pebbles. Here the Little Tern has at last been

**Below left** Active conservation often involves strenuous maintenance. These volunteers are busily planting trees in an area that has been previously felled, in an effort to attract different species of birds.

**Left** Whooping Cranes have been the subject of one of the most intensive conservation projects ever. After years of slow decline, a captive breeding and egg translocation programme has established a secondary population in the U S. These birds are at their traditional wintering zone in Aransas.

persuaded away from the beach. Avocets breed alongside Common and Sandwich Terns.

## Species protection

Conservation does, however, also concern itself with species protection, especially with migrant birds that may need a chain of sanctuaries where they can find refuge. The Whooping Crane of North America seemed doomed to extinction despite all the efforts made to protect the last two or three dozen birds. Nesting among the wild marshes of Canada's Wood Buffalo National Park, where protection activities would probably do more harm than good, these splendid birds then made a length-of-the-continent migration to winter along the Gulf Coast at the Aransas Sanctuary in Texas. Over the years the migrating birds were accompanied by watchful aircraft to ensure that

they were not shot up by misguided sportsmen. Yet, year after year, numbers see-sawed around in a steadily declining population. In desperation, a captive breeding flock was established and a new population created. At the time of writing the gamble would appear to have paid off and the number of Cranes seems to be on the increase.

In Britain, the Red Kite was once down to a handful of birds based in the remote valleys of central Wales. Slowly and painfully the number has increased by dint of the devoted work in nest-guarding of a small band of enthusiasts. Today the Kite would seem secure, but every year nests are robbed of their eggs so that some idiot can gloat over them in a cabinet.

These are just two examples of what has been achieved in two different continents.

There is no end to what needs to be done.

# GLOSSARY

**Adaption**: the way in which a bird has changed to meet the circumstances in which it finds itself.

**Adult**: a bird that has acquired its full plumage. To be compared with juvenile or immature plumages.

**Aquatic**: a life-style associated with water.

**Avian**: relating to birds.

**Axilliaries**: a group of feathers located where the underwing meets the body - the "armpits".

**Bar**: a mark across a feather or group of feathers (see Stripe).

**Belly**: underparts of a bird between breast and undertail coverts.

**Bend of the wing**: the point where the wing changes from extending forward to extending backward.

**Cere**: a bare patch at the base of the bill in such groups as birds of prey and Parrots.

**Clutch**: the eggs of a bird in its nest.

**Coniferous**: cone-bearing trees, usually evergreen.

**Conspecific**: where two (or more) differing birds belong to one species.

**Coverts**: groups of small feathers that cover the base of the major flight feathers, e.g. wing coverts, tail coverts.

**Crepuscular**: active at dawn and dusk.

**Crest**: extended feathers on crown.

**Deciduous**: broad-leafed trees that shed their leaves.

**Decurved**: down-curved.

**Emarginated**: wing feather that narrows on the outer edge.

**Ethology**: study of behaviour in the natural environment.

**Extinct**: no longer in existence.

**Feral**: domestic forms that have gone wild.

**Field Guide**: a book of bird identification for a specific area.

**Flanks**: sides of the body below the folded wings.

**Frontal**: on the forehead.

**Gamebirds**: birds hunted for sport or food.

**Gregarious**: birds that form flocks.

**Gular**: throat.

**Insectivorous**: birds that eat insects.

**Juvenile**: the plumage in which young birds leave the nest.

**Lores**: area between the bill and the eye.

**Mandibles**: the two parts of a bird's bill.

**Moult**: the process of shedding feathers and replacing them.

**Nape**: hind neck.

**Nocturnal**: active at night.

**Omnivorous**: birds that eat a wide range of foods.

**Oologist**: egg collector.

**Pelagic**: birds that live in the open ocean.

**Phase**: plumage differences within a single species.

**Preen**: a bird's method of feather care and maintenance with its bill.

**Primaries**: the outer flight feathers that act as the means of propulsion.

**Race**: sub-species.

**Raptor**: bird of prey.

**Rump**: area of body above the tail.

**Scapulars**: feathers that cover the area where the upperwing joins the body.

**Secondaries**: group of inner flight feathers responsible for lift.

**Shorebird**: wader; term usually used in North America.

**Species**: a group of birds that are capable of interbreeding to produce fertile young and that do not usually breed with others.

**Speculum**: patch on upper wing of ducks.

**Stripe**: lengthwise mark on feather or group of feathers (see Bar).

**Subspecies**: a group of birds within a species that can be distinguished from other groups.

**Tarsus**: leg bone immediately above the foot.

**Tertials**: wing feathers between secondaries and body.

**Thermal**: rising column of warm air; used by soaring birds.

**Vernacular**: English name as opposed to scientific name.

**Wader**: term used in Britain for shorebird; in North America refers to Herons, Egrets and Ibis.

**Wildfow**: Ducks, Geese and Swans.

# INDEX

Page numbers in **bold** refer to illustrations

# ACKNOWLEDGMENTS

Quarto would like to thank the following for providing photographs
and for permission to reproduce copyright material:

37 (left) National Sound Archive/British Library of Wildlife
Sounds/Richard Ranst 70 ARDEA 71 Jack Skill.
All other photographs supplied by Bruce Coleman.